MIGHTY MINI-PLAYS

For the German Classroom

By
Patti Lozano

Translated by
Renate Donovan

12 Short Humorous Plays For Intermediate Levels

Dolo Publications, Inc.

The cover illustration was created by Carmen Plott.

Copyright ©Patti Lozano 1998
All Rights Reserved
First Printing 1998
Printed in the United States of America

ISBN 0-9650980-4-4

This publication is protected by Copyright and permission should be obtained from the publisher prior to any prohibited reproduction, storage in a retrieval system, or transmission in any form or by any means, electronic, mechanical, photocopying, recording or otherwise. Permission for duplication, however, is granted to the individual teacher for any portions of the book that will benefit the student in his/her classroom.

Clip art provided by Corel Gallery Magic, Corel Corporation © 1997

Dolo Publications, Inc.
18315 Spruce Creek Drive
Houston, Texas 77084
Toll Free: (800)830-1460
fax: (281)679-9092 or (281)463-4808
Email: orders@dololanguages.com or plozano@sbcglobal.net
www.dololanguages.com

Acknowledgements...

Heartfelt thanks go to...
 my husband Alberto for listening to and scrutinizing each plot and dialogue many, many times!
 to my mother for her infinite support, endless enthusiasm and inexhaustable editing endeavors!
 to Renate Donovan for her passionate interest and linguistic skills in translating these plays from Spanish to German!
 to Dr. Veronika Wilson and Carolyn Zerbe for their very valuable time and considerable competence in additional editing of the German manuscript and very useful suggestions pertaining to current usage!
 to Barbara Lasater, a wonderful actor and acting coach for young people, for sharing her experiences and expertise with me!

Dedication...

 Mom, this book is for you!

Other works by Patti Lozano
(Published by Dolo Publications, Inc.)

Music that teaches Spanish!
More music that teaches Spanish!
Leyendas con canciones
Mighty Mini-Plays for the Spanish Classroom
Mighty Mini-Plays for the French Classroom
Mighty Mini-Plays for the ESL Classroom
Music That Teaches English!
Music That Teaches French!
Music That Teaches German!
Get Them Talking!
Spanish Grammar Swings!
French Grammar Swings!
Teatro de Cuentos de Hadas
Latin American Legends: on Page, on Stage & in Song
Skinny Skits
Petites Pièces de Théâtre
Winzige Theaterstücke
Let's Chat!

Table of Contents

ACT I
Previews

Synopses and Language Objectives	i
Introduction	v
Introduction (How to Use this Book!)	vii
Introduction (Optional Acting Tips)	xi

ACT II
Mighty Mini-Plays Overviews and Scripts

1. Ärger in der Geographiestunde	1
2. Kanal PAN-ORAMA	7
3. Das Verlorene Buch	13
4. Marlene	19
5. Das Ideale Haustier	25
6. Die Geburtstagsfeier	31
7. Arno Verliebt Sich	37
8. Reisesachen	43
9. "Wir Kochen Heute mit Karl und Karoline"	49
10. Ein Nachmittag mit Drei Freunden	57
11. Frühstück für Fritz	63
12. Hausarbeiten	71

ACT III

Workshops Offered	79
Ordering Information	81

Mighty Mini-Plays Synopses and Language Objectives

1. ## Ärger in der Geographiestunde
   Synopsis: *Frau Schwab is attempting to teach her German class, but the class keeps shrinking as the principal, Herr Zimmer, takes more and more students away to other classes and activities.*
   Language Objectives:
   Vocabulary: classroom objects, school classes, classrooms, school personnel
   Structures: simple present tense sentences

2. ## Kanal PAN-ORAMA
   Synopsis: *Herr Wetar, television weather anchor for Kanal PAN-ORAMA, with mounting discontent, checks in with his weather correspondents around the world.*
   Language Objectives:
   Vocabulary: weather expressions
   Structures: related phrases

3. ## Das Verlorene Buch
   Synopsis: *Georg searches his house in vain for his missing library book as his family waits impatiently to leave for the library.*
   Language Objectives:
   Vocabulary: objects and furniture in the home
   Structures: auxiliary verbs, prepositions

4. ## Marlene
   Synopsis: *Two simpleminded young men meet a beautiful stranger in the park. They try to coax her into conversation, but she talks about her car in rapturous, mechanical phrases.*
   Language Objectives:
   Vocabulary: nature
   Structures: present tense verb conjugations

Mighty Mini-Plays Synopses and Language Objectives... *continued*

5. Das Ideale Haustier
Synopsis: *Renate goes to the pet store to buy the perfect animal companion.*
Language Objectives:
  Vocabulary: domesticated animals
  Structures: descriptive adjectives

6. Die Geburtstagsfeier
Synopsis: *Max tries valiantly against all odds to attend Frieda's 16th birthday party but he arrives too late... or is it too early?*
Language Objectives:
  Vocabulary: time expressions, transportation
  Structures: separable prefix verbs

7. Arno Verliebt Sich
Synopsis: *Arno tries every way possible to get Anna to notice him, but she is only interested in her book about cats.*
Language Objectives:
  Vocabulary: parts of the body
  Structures: descriptive adjective agreement

8. Reisesachen
Synopsis: *Frau Knopf, the clothing store owner, and her employee, Ursula, desperately try to sell their frugal customer, Herr Baum, the amazing "One-Fabric-Does-All" clothing.*
Language Objectives:
  Vocabulary: articles of clothing
  Structures: commands

9. "Wir Kochen Heute mit Karl und Karoline"
Synopsis: *Karl and Karoline are the enthusiastic hosts of the wildly popular and moronic TV cooking show, "**Wir Kochen Heute mit Karl und Karoline!**" Join them today as they discuss and compare fruits as well as answer inane questions from their fervent, dimwitted studio audience.*
Language Objectives:
  Vocabulary: fruits
  Structures: utility verbs in plural form, related to cooking

Mighty Mini-Plays Synopses and Language Objectives... *continued*

10. Ein Nachmittag mit Drei Freunden
   Synopsis: *Experience the delightful, mundane adventures of three friends one sunny afternoon.*
   Language Objectives:
   Vocabulary: adjectives
   Structures: comparatives and superlatives

11. Frühstück für Fritz
   Synopsis: *Eva has the dubious pleasure of serving breakfast to Herr Hansen and his annoying "friend," Fritz.*
   Language Objectives:
   Vocabulary: breakfast foods
   Structures: common phrases for ordering and dining out in a restaurant, use of auxiliary verbs (modals)

12. Hausarbeiten
   Synopsis: *Mom requests help with the chores, but everyone in the family is too busy. Mom has the final revenge.*
   Language Objectives:
   Vocabulary: chores to be done around the home
   Structures: commands

INTRODUCTION 1: About the introduction

Read this introduction! This is a fun introduction to read. I wrote it in an entertaining style specifically so you will read it! Personally, I don't usually take the time to read textbook introductions, but I would definitely read this one, perhaps over coffee or while lying in a hammock (because it *is* fun.)

If you are in a hurry to get to the plays, go ahead and skip over the serious (i.e. instructionally informative) "**INTRODUCTION 2**" as well as the inspirational, heartwarming "**INTRODUCTION 3.**" Jump ahead all the way to the "**INTRODUCTION 4,**" because it is really important, useful and, well, fun!

INTRODUCTION 2: About this book

Mighty Mini-Plays is not lofty drama. It bears scarce resemblance to the revered works of Schiller or Dürrenmatt, and probably ought not even share the same bookshelf space with the mighty Goethe! Think of **Mighty Mini-Plays** as "*Saturday Night Live* Meets the German Classroom." In other words, these short plays will not teach your students an everlasting appreciation of classical theater, but they will allow your students to have a marvelously fun time as they act and speak together to bring first and second year German vocabulary and structures to life in ridiculous everyday situations.

Mighty Mini-Plays contains the scripts to twelve mini-productions. You may consider them to be either very short complete plays or very lengthy developed skits. At any rate, all skits are written to be 15 - 20 minutes in length when performed.

The plots and style of dialogue are written to intrigue and entertain middle and high school age students. Several situations deal with pursuit of the opposite sex, some deal with crises at home or in school, and others are parodies of news or talk shows on television.

All plays are meticulously written in present tense. I have given serious attention to keep the conversation flowing naturally in the present tense, even while alluding to events in the past and future. Cases such as the imperfect, progressive and subjunctive are not used, even when they are standard fare in requesting, hoping, explaining and remembering situations. As frequently as possible, I have used auxiliary verbs to indicate the future, a wish, or to create a mood. The reader will find many instances of *möchten, werden, wollen, sollen* and *können* throughout the book. This might occasionally cause a sentence to seem a bit simplistic. Please understand the reason: it is not that my editors or

I do not have command of the spoken language, but that we are determined for these plays to be simple in structure, yet advanced in critical thinking and social skills. **Mighty Mini-plays** *are instructionally appropriate for late-first year German students with the support of the classroom teachers as well as second year students working in small groups on their own with minimal assistance.*

All pages in the **Mighty Mini-Plays** *text are fully reproducible.*

INTRODUCTION 3: How the plays began

For five years I served as television teacher for an elementary Spanish long-distance program in Houston, Texas. I designed the lessons, wrote the scripts, composed the songs, created the props, taught the Spanish, trained the guest performers, worked the puppets and acted as myself and in other roles in over 250 episodes. (In case you are wondering by now, no, I was not the camera man or the producer.)

Ours was a five year, sequential program. We began the first lesson for first grade with the words, "Buenos días" and a song. For the first three years we taught basic first year Spanish vocabulary and simple structures in a fabricated rainforest set with lush plastic vegetation, mangy fake grass and tropical Carribean-looking paper maché parrots hanging everywhere. Strategically placed in this tropical paradise were easels, dry erase boards, felt boards, maps and other equipment common to a language classroom. To capture the interest of my students in classroom video land, I began each day's lesson with a short, silly skit followed by a song. Several puppet companions assisted me daily: a naïve wolf, a highstrung cow and a depressed toucan. Later many more of their friends joined the show. The puppets' distinct personalities developed as the show evolved, which helped me to create skits geared to their individual eccentricities.

By fourth grade, my students needed to put all this vocabulary and structure to practical use, thus our video program consisted of a year-long hypothetical trip to Mexico, ostensibly to search for my annoying iguana puppet's family. Thanks to a federal grant, we were able to use Chroma Key footage, which made it appear as if we really were *climbing the ruins of Tenochtitlán or ordering a meal in a Guadalajaran restaurant, with mariachis strumming their guitars in the background.*

In the fifth grade it was decided that the videos really needed to get students ready for the more structurally oriented language classes of middle and high school. I chose to write a 15 - 20 minute skit, (a "mini-play!") for each video lesson. Each play explored and stressed certain language concepts. Spanish-speaking teacher aides worked with the students in the classrooms before and after they viewed each video to practice targeted vocabulary and structures introduced in that week's lesson.

Now, fifth graders (on up) for the most part do not want to see videos with roles acted by adorable puppets, at least not in public. (I do happen to know personally, having raised a fifth grader, that in the privacy of their own home, they still are tremendously entertained by the Sesame Street brand of humor, which can actually be quite sophisticated.) Pre-adolescents and adolescents through high school love absurd humor, ludicrous and incongruent humor, the humor that one sees on *Saturday Night Live, Mr. Bean* and old *Monty Python* sketches.

My goal was to write 15 - 20 minute long plays that: 1) reinforced the students' Spanish by utilizing familiar structures and vocabulary, 2) were relevant to the students' lives by dealing with everyday issues and occurrences, and 3) held their interest via humorous plots and dialogues with unexpected endings. I often wrote guest roles for student actors who had studied Spanish through this video program, with the result that the phrases had to be fairly simple and direct. Many times the Spanish teachers acted in videos as well!

Because middle school teachers requested the use of these videos in their classrooms, I wrote age-appropriate dialogue and plot line for fifth grade through high school students. This final year of videos was extremely successful and popular with students and teachers alike.

Soon after I heard that teachers were taking my scripts from the videos and adapting them for their classrooms for events such as student assemblies, P.T.A. meetings, summer programs and even just for classroom fun. At first I simply felt flattered, but soon my agitated mind, which is always searching for new projects, thought: why not adapt these skits, add stage directions and make these available to all Spanish, French and German teachers? I eventually chose the twelve favorite video plays of the year, spent nine months rewriting them, adapting them and field testing them in schools, and finally **Mighty Mini-Plays** was born!

Renate Donovan, my mother and a native Austrian, foreign language coordinator and former German teacher, then translated all the plays, taking special care to also change all data to that which is pertinent to German teachers and students.

I hope you and your students have as much fun rehearsing and performing these plays as we did!

INTRODUCTION 4: (The important part) How to use this book!
Organization

Each of the twelve plays includes an **Overview** page followed by the script, which is five or six pages long.

The Overview Page

This page, which is written specifically for the teacher's use, contains the sections: **Synopsis, Language Objectives, Production Notes, How to Extend** or **Reduce the Length of the Play** and **Staging Suggestions**. It shares information and insights that the teacher may want to consider before casting the characters and staging the play. Students do not receive a copy of this page.

☆ Synopsis

The synopsis contains very short summary of the following play. Every plot has some kind of unexpected twist at the end, designed to surprise and amuse both the actors and the audience, (and you, the teacher, of course!) Sometimes the synopsis describes the plot twist and other times it keeps it under wraps. You may, or may not want to share the synopsis with your students.

☆ Instructional Objectives

Usually instructional objectives are listed for both vocabulary and structures and often examples are cited. (Remember: the purpose of **Mighty Mini-Plays** is not to teach new concepts, but to reinforce what has already been introduced during classroom instruction!) For this reason, target vocabulary and structures are not pounded mercilessly into the students' conscience through every spoken dramatic line, but appear occasionally, as they would be spoken in the context of a natural conversation.

Almost every word spoken in these mini-plays is standard first and second year German vocabulary from any middle or high school basal text. Whenever a slightly unusual word is used, an asterik (*) follows it, and an English definition, written in the order of appearance in the text, may be found on the final page of that particular mini-play.

☆ Production Notes

The Production Notes provide helpful miscellaneous tips to the teacher, or perhaps in this case we should now bestow upon you the title of "director!" The information in the Production Notes varies, but it is always very important. Make sure you read it before developing the play. Sometimes the style of the play is explained or acting "tips" are suggested for a particular character. Sometimes insights to a character's personality are explored. Often there are suggestions for casting, for creating props and optional backdrops.

★ How To Extend The Length Of The Play

This section gives you several suggestions for each play on how to add to the performance length of the play by creating dialogue for additional subplots, characters and situations. There are several situations in which you might want to use the "How to Extend the Length of the Play" section:

✓ You are performing for the student body, P.T.A, elementary school or whatever, and need a full-length play.

✓ You wish to engage all the students in your classroom in the same play and need roles for all students.

✓ You want to further reinforce certain vocabulary and structures through additional dialogue.

There are several ways to create additional dialogue:

✓ You, the teacher, may sit at home in your most creativity-inspiring room with your most creativity-inspired drink and snack in front of you and try your hand as a playwright.

✓ Students, either individually or in small groups may be given a finite length of time to compose dialogue. Each student or group may audition this dialogue with the class, and the students may vote to decide which dialogue will be added to the play.

✓ The class may add dialogue as a large group with the teacher as facilitator and supreme director.

★ How To Reduce The Length Of The Play

At other times you may need to reduce the length of the play for several reasons. For example:

✓ Your students are presenting the play for a competition and have a seven minute performance time limit.

✓ You want your students to memorize the play and you wish to delete a certain amount of dialogue.

✓ You want smaller rehearsing and performing student groups.

In this case suggestions are given for reducing characters' lines without losing the flow and meaning of the plot and sometimes for deleting entire characters. You will instruct students to use a marker to cross out the deleted dialogue on their script copies.

★ Staging Suggestions

Let's talk about the pitifully rendered sketches at the bottom of most

Overview pages. Why, you ask, did the author create such lovely, vibrant stories in such a thoughtful format, and then allow such mediocre artwork? The truth is that the playwright (that's me) is first a teacher, secondly a musician and thirdly (and only in a very broad stretch of the word) an actor. Nowhere in my resumé does the title "artist" appear. These primitive drawings exist to give you an idea of the staging I use when performing these skits with students both in classroom settings and school cafeteria/auditorium stages. The drawings represent the placement of students "At Rise," which is an impressive theatrical term that means "when the play begins." Staging directions for student movement after the play begins is always written in italics as it occurs in the dialogue.

Occasionally you are mercifully spared the Staging Suggestions illustration; this happens in the mini-plays where the setting is largely imaginary or optional.

The Script

☆ Characters

The characters are always listed, with a minimum of description, in the order of appearance. The students may "flesh" out their roles depending on whether or not you want to get into the true essence of theater arts (as opposed to the true essence of German classroom instruction). The roles for the most part are quite generic. Usually girls can play boys' roles and vice versa. Most roles are designed for the 11 - 16 year old's thought processes and maturity level. Read through the entire play before casting parts to make sure you do not assign anyone anything particularly embarrassing to him or her. Most plays have roles for 4 - 5 students, but you may always create more roles or omit them, if necessary.

☆ Setting

Mighty Mini-Plays do not need any elaborate staging! Our goal is not Broadway, but fluid communication. The amount of setting is really up to you and your students. When the play calls for a sofa, if you have a sofa in your classroom, then great! If not, just drape some chairs with a comforter to approximate a sofa. A doorway may be a long piece of brown butcher paper. News anchor desks, TV cooking show countertops and diner counters may all be created with plain fold-up tables. A few plastic potted plants can make a great image of a woodsy park. (I know this from my extensive experience in dense, plastic tropical rainforest sets!) Old linen bedsheets that are painted and butcher paper that is decorated make wonderful optional backdrops that enhance certain moods or create locations.

★ Props

The number of props used in the plays varies tremendously. One play entitled *"Marlene,"* (actually the most intricate one of them all) only requires two pinecones as props. Other plays need a great deal of sundry, seemingly unrelated items. You should not have to purchase any props. Have volunteers bring items from home for the Spanish class to use for the duration of the play.

It is important to gather all props together in a box before the first rehearsal. Always read through the play to make sure you have all the necessary props, and also to determine where they must be placed for actors to grab them as they need them during the performance.

★ "AT RISE"

"AT RISE" gives you the exact location and occupation of each actor as the play starts. It is also a very impressive, professional-sounding drama word to insert nonchalantly into conversation from time to time.

★ Costumes

Sorry, no costumes. We have enough to do as language teachers, without worrying about costumes! If your students want to wear something special for their role (and some undoubtedly will,) that's just great, but it's between you and them. If costumes really excite you, browse through your local assistance ministry and charity stores, as well as garage sales and flea markets for great costume clothes at next-to-nothing prices.

INTRODUCTION 5: Acting Tips (This section is optional!)

If you have read the introduction up to this point, you have now the essential information necessary to develop these mini-plays with your students. If you are eager and anxious to immediately begin your rehearsal, skip this section and jump on to the first play, which is entitled *"Ärger in der Geographiestunde."* However, if you have become inspired and the bright lights of Broadway beckon you, take a moment more to read the following acting tips.

Actually you and I are already actors. We act every day as we teach second languages. We act as we teach nouns, verbs, adjectives, prepositions, expressions and just about everything. We hold our students' attention because we are interesting to watch. (I'm not sure I like how that sentence came out.) The following are some additional acting tips that I've learned from my years as instructional video teacher and actor, and by listening to my three school-age sons, who are all very active in community theater.

ACTING TIPS

1. ***Acting is believing.*** You are not only playing the role of the Martyred Mother, the Frantic Suitor, the Perky Waitress or the Angry Customer. You become that person. You step into their skin and feel what it's like to be someone else.

2. ***Acting is a voice.*** Always project your voice to the back of the theater (or auditorium, cafeteria or classroom.) Try to make your voice flexible: experiment with intensity, pitch and rhythm. Enhance emotions with exaggerated inflections. Always make sure your words are clear and distinct, especially your beginning and ending consonants.

3. ***Acting is thought.*** Think about the meaning of your lines, no matter how many times you say them. Say your lines more slowly than you do in real life because your audience needs time to digest your information. Remember that you've heard your lines many times, but your audience only gets the opportunity to make sense of your words once.

4. ***Acting is movement.*** All action on the stage should be "big!" Emphasize your words and actions with gestures and movement. Do not make unnecessary movements like scratching your face or tapping your foot, because the audience will watch that instead of the story.

5. ***Acting is focus.*** Always focus on the character to whom you are talking. Always make eye contact with him or her, unless the director or script instructs you otherwise.

6. ***Acting is creativity.*** You are often given very little insight into your character. (This is especially true in short works, such as mini-plays!) Use your imagination to create your character. What does she do in her leisure time?

What kind of temperament does he have?

Create the physical aspects of your character as well. What kind of walk does she have? Does he slouch on a couch or sit ramrod straight? Does he sigh a lot, sniff daintily, or clear his throat loudly?

7. ***Acting is fun!*** *This is the final and most important advice! Acting is fun because it allows you to step out of your skin and be someone else for a little while. Acting lets you react to situations and people in unusual ways without fear of reprisal. Acting is the joy of the feel and power of words, as Shakespeare said it so well, "...trippingly on the tongue." Acting is speaking with strangers who become friends as you work and play together to perfect a scene. Acting is creating a fine art out of the everyday process of communication.*

I have only one more bit of advice for you now, and that is for you and your students to "BREAK A LEG!" when you perform these mini-plays, and always have a great time doing so!

1. Ärger in der Geographiestunde
⬤ Overview ⬤

SYNOPSIS: Frau Schwab is attempting to teach her German class, but the class keeps shrinking as the principal, Herr Zimmer takes more and more students away to various other classes and activities.

LANGUAGE OBJECTIVES:
   Vocabulary: classroom objects, school classes, classrooms, school personnel
   Structures: simple present tense sentences

PRODUCTION NOTES:
   FRAU SCHWAB has the most demanding role with many lines to memorize. She may want to hold a "roll book" in her hands during the play in order to hide her script.
   All roles in this play may be played by either boys or girls.

TO EXTEND THE LENGTH OF THE PLAY:
   Create additional roles for students in Frau Schwab's classroom, along with additional reasons for interruptions and removal of students from the German classroom. Add more classroom objects, school personnel and school courses to the script.

TO REDUCE THE LENGTH OF THE PLAY:
   Omit one or more of the student characters from the script.

STAGING SUGGESTION:

1. Ärger in der Geographiestunde

CHARACTERS: 8 Actors
    FRAU SCHWAB (the German teacher)
    Students: (PETER, KARL, OTTO, JULIA, MITZI, MARIA)
    HERR ZIMMER (the principal)

SETTING: A classroom with a chalkboard, teacher desk, 6 student desks and a door

PROPS: chalk, eraser, large map of Europe, pointer, clipboard, textbooks, a tennis racket

AT RISE: *FRAU SCHWAB, the German teacher, is standing at the front of her classroom. The students are seated in chairs at desks in front of her. A large map of Europe is displayed on the wall or chalk board next to her.*

FRAU SCHWAB: Guten Morgen, liebe Schüler. Heute lernen wir etwas über die Länder Europas und ihren Hauptstädten. Dazu braucht ihr eure Geographiebücher und ihre Landkarten.

KARL (*Raises hand*)

FRAU SCHWAB: Ja, Karl?

KARL: Ach, Frau Schwab, ich hab' mein Geographiebuch nicht dabei.

FRAU SCHWAB: Also, Karl, wo ist denn dein Geographiebuch?

KARL: Ich weiss es nicht — aber hier habe ich mein Mathematikbuch!

FRAU SCHWAB: Das hilft dir nicht! Das ist nicht die Mathestunde, sondern die Geographiestunde.

KARL: Es tut mir leid, Frau Schwab.

FRAU SCHWAB: Mitzi, wo hast du denn dein Geographiebuch? (*Pauses and watches as KARL moves noisily next to MITZI*) Gut. Heute lernen wir etwas über die Länder Europas und ihre Hauptstädte. Ihr wisst bereits, dass dieser grosse Kontinent Europa heisst. Also, (*Scans class*) Maria, wie heisst dieses Land?

1.2

MARIA (*Unsure*): Ist das Österreich?

FRAU SCHWAB: Ja, sehr gut. Und wie heisst die Hauptstadt von Österreich? (*Interrupted by a knock at the door*) Herein, bitte.

HERR ZIMMER (*Enters, students suddenly sit straighter, FRAU SCHWAB becomes a bit nervous and formal*)

FRAU SCHWAB: Ah, Herr Zimmer! Was für eine Überraschung!*

HERR ZIMMER: Frau Schwab, bitte entschuldigen Sie. Ich will Ihren Unterricht nicht unterbrechen, aber, ist —(*Consults clipboard*) Maria Schmitt in dieser Klasse?

FRAU SCHWAB: Ja, sie ist hier.

HERR ZIMMER: Maria, deine Mutter ist in meinem Büro. Du hast einen wichtigen* Termin*...

MARIA: Ach, ja. Ich habe einen Termin beim Zahnarzt. Tschüs, Frau Schwab. Wir sehen uns morgen wieder. (*Gathers books and exits*)

FRAU SCHWAB (*Calls after her*): Maria, nimm dein Geobuch mit. Du kannst deine Aufgabe beim Zahnarzt lesen. - Otto, beantworte du die Frage.

OTTO (*Hesitates*): Welche Frage?

FRAU SCHWAB: Die Frage lautet: "Wie heisst die Hauptstadt von Österreich?"

OTTO: Es tut mir leid. Das weiss ich nicht. Auf welcher Seite im Buch sind wir denn?

FRAU SCHWAB: Otto, du musst aufpassen. Wir sind auf Seite 156.

OTTO: Danke, Frau Schwab. (*Finds page and reads*) Die Hauptstadt von Frankreich ist Paris.

FRAU SCHWAB: Sehr gut, Otto, aber die Frage lautet: "Wie heisst die Hauptstadt von Österreich?"

OTTO (*Prepares to answer when he is interrupted by another knock*)

FRAU SCHWAB (*A bit annoyed*): Ja, bitte, herein!

HERR ZIMMER (*Enters, students once again sit up straighter, FRAU SCHWAB looks perplexed*)

FRAU SCHWAB: Guten Tag, Herr Zimmer - was nun?

HERR ZIMMER: Bitte entschuldigen Sie! Ich will nicht schon wieder stören, aber — (*Consults his clipboard*) ist Otto Herman in Ihrer Klasse?

FRAU SCHWAB: Ja, er ist hier.

1.3

HERR ZIMMER: Sehr gut. Otto, bitte komm mit in die Sporthalle. Wir wollen das Tennisteam photographieren.

OTTO: Das sind die Bilder für das Jahrbuch, nicht wahr?

HERR ZIMMER: Ja. *(Glances at his watch)* In zehn Minuten soll es losgehen.

OTTO: Dann brauche ich meinen Tennisschläger. *(Gets tennis racket from under desk - asks classmates)* Wie sieht meine Frisur* aus? Bis morgen, Frau Schwab. Tschüs! *(Runs out)*

FRAU SCHWAB: *(Calls after him)* Aber Otto, wie heisst die Hauptstadt von - *(The door slams, silence, then FRAU SCHWAB says dryly)* Die Hauptstadt von Österreich heisst Wien. (Sighs) Also, machen wir weiter. Hier seht ihr ein Land in der Mitte des Kontinents. *(Points to Germany)*. Wie heisst es denn, Peter?

PETER *(Flustered because he hasn't been paying attention):* Ah — ich heisse Peter.

FRAU SCHWAB: Was sagst du da? Nein, Peter, nicht "Wie heisst **du**?" sondern "Wie heisst dieses Land?"

PETER: Ach so — *(Thinks hard)* Ist es __ Deutschland?

FRAU SCHWAB: Ja! Das ist Deutschland. *(To class)* Und, wer weiss, welche die Hauptstadt von Deutschland ist?

PETER *(Raises hand and waves enthusiastically)*

FRAU SCHWAB: Ja, Peter.

PETER: Wird die Basketballmannschaft heute auch noch photographiert?

FRAU SCHWAB: Peter, dies hier ist nicht die Sportstunde. Ich weiss es nicht. Du bist in der Geographiestunde. Nun, nochmals, welche ist — *(Once again interrupted by knocking, she calls out angrily)* Wer ist da?

HERR ZIMMER: Bitte entschuldigen Sie, Frau Schwab. Ich will nicht schon wieder stören *(Chuckles, oblivious to FRAU SCHWAB's frustration)*, aber ist — *(Consults clipboard)* Peter Heller in Ihrer Klasse?

FRAU SCHWAB: Ja, er ist hier.

HERR ZIMMER: Peter, wir haben ein Problem mit deiner Mathematikprüfung. Du muss sofort zu deinem Mathelehrer. Bring dein Mathematikbuch, dein Heft, deinen Bleistift, und deinen Rechner mit.

PETER: Ja, Herr Zimmer.

1.4

FRAU SCHWAB *(Watches dejectedly as PETER exits, looks at three students left in class, and then asks with forced brightness)*: Also, Julia, welche Stadt ist die Hauptstadt von Deutschland?

JULIA *(Reads aloud from textbook)*: Deutschland ist ein Land in Europa.

FRAU SCHWAB: Richtig, Julia. Aber, wie heisst die Hauptstadt von Deutschland?

JULIA: Die Hauptstadt von Deutschland heisst - *(Is interrupted as the door flies open)*

HERR ZIMMER *(Enters frantically)*: Pardon, Frau Schwab. Ich will Sie nicht schon wieder stören, aber ist — *(Consults clipboard)* Julia Schwarz in dieser Klasse?

FRAU SCHWAB *(Taken aback)*: Ja, sie ist hier.

HERR ZIMMER *(Breathlessly, waving arms)*: Komm schnell in den Biologieraum. Da ist vielleicht was los! Dein Experiment! Komm schnell!

JULIA *(Jumps out of seat, with sudden fear)*: Herr Zimmer, ist was mit meinen Schlangen los?

HERR ZIMMER: Genau! *(Breathes deeply, tries to compose himself)* Deine Schlangen sind nicht mehr im Terrarium. Sie sind überall, auf den Schreibtischen, in den Computern. . . und gleich sind sie auch noch in der Cafeteria und in der Bibliothek.

JULIA: Ach, wie schrecklich! Meine Schlangen! Tschüs, Frau Schwab.
(JULIA and HERR ZIMMER exit quickly)

KARL *(Springs to life, jumps up out of his seat)*: Schlangen! Wirklich? Furchtbar!* Jetzt sind sie in der Cafeteria? Ich muss sie sehen! Julia, warte auf mich! Ich geh' mit dir. *(Runs to door, stops, turns to FRAU SCHWAB)*: Entschuldigen Sie mich, bitte. Bis morgen. *(Exits)*

FRAU SCHWAB *(Pauses and regards her one remaining, and very attentive, student)*: Mitzi, wie heisst die Hauptstadt von Deutschland?

MITZI *(Raises hand self-importantly)*

FRAU SCHWAB *(Exasperated)*: Mitzi, warum meldest* du dich? Schau dir unsere Geoklasse an. Es sind keine anderen Schüler mehr hier! Maria ist im Büro, Otto ist in der Sporthalle, Peter ist in der Matheklasse,

Julia ist im Bioraum, und wer weiss wo Karl ist? Schau, Mitzi, du bist die einzige Schülerin in der Geographieklasse ... und deshalb frage ich dich — wie heisst die Hauptstadt von Deutschland?

MITZI *(Looks around):* Oh. *(Stands up majestically with book)* Frau Schwab, die Hauptstadt von Deutschland ist — *(Interrupted by the bell)* Ach! Die Pausenklingel! Die Geographiestunde ist vorbei! Jetzt habe ich Geschichte. *(Exits)*

FRAU SCHWAB *(Speaks to the empty chairs, points to the map):* Sie heisst Berlin ... die Hauptstadt von Deutschland heisst Berlin!

DAS ENDE

WORTSCHATZ (in order of appearance in the play)

Ärger, der (title)	*interruption, annoyance*
wichtig	*important*
Überraschung, die	*surprise*
Termin, der	*date, appointment*
Frisur, die	*hairdo*
furchtbar	*awful*
sich melden	*to ask to speak*

2. Kanal PAN-ORAMA
✣ Overview ✣

SYNOPSIS: Otto Wetar, television weather anchor for Kanal PAN-ORAMA checks in with his weather correspondents around the world.

> **LANGUAGE OBJECTIVES:**
> Vocabulary: weather expressions
> Structures: related phrases

PRODUCTION NOTES:

The focal point of the "stage" is the anchor desk. An attractive sign, hung either behind or from the desk, announces "Kanal PAN-ORAMA."

Other areas of the classroom or stage represent the beach in Capri, Italy, a ski resort in Zermatt, Switzerland, and a park in Vienna, Austria. Posters, signs and/or props, such as beach towels, heavy jackets and so on may be displayed to designate each area.

TO EXTEND THE LENGTH OF THE PLAY:

Add more news correspondents in other parts of Europe, reporting additional weather patterns.
Add roles for cameramen in Chicago and in remote locations.

TO REDUCE THE LENGTH OF THE PLAY:

Delete the role of one or more reporters.

STAGING SUGGESTION:

2. Kanal PAN-ORAMA

CHARACTERS: 5 Actors
    OTTO WETAR (Kanal PAN-ORAMA proud weather anchor)
    JUTTA HEITER (visiting cousin from Munich, Germany)
    TARA BRAUN (Capri, Italy weather correspondent)
    JÜRGEN HOCH (Zermatt, Switzerland weather correspondent)
    KURT GRASS (Vienna, Austria weather correspondent)

SETTING: A news anchor desk with a large Kanal PAN-ORAMA sign, various areas of the classroom decorated with signs, posters and/or props to represent: a sunny resort in Capri, Italy, a trendy ski resort in Zermatt, Switzerland, a park in Vienna, Austria

PROPS: OTTO WETAR and JUTTA HEITER each need: earphones, suitcase, a few items of miscellaneous clothing to hastily pack. OTTO WETAR also needs papers to shuffle. TARA BRAUN: microphone, sun lotion, sunglasses; JÜRGEN HOCH: microphone, huge plate of food, a large drink. KURT GRASS: microphone and a sun visor

AT RISE: *OTTO WETAR is seated behind PAN-ORAMA anchor desk, shuffling his weather report papers. JUTTA HEITER is seated next to him. Their suitcases and extra clothing are hidden under the desk, their earphones lie on the anchor desk in front of them.*

OTTO WETAR *(Talking to camera in a jovial, resounding anchorman voice):*
Ich heisse Otto Wetter und bin der Metereologe hier im Kanal PAN-ORAMA, ihr Lieblingskanal, der Kanal, der Ihnen täglich Europas Wetter berichtet. Heute ist es mir ein Vergnügen Ihnen meine Kusine, Jutta Heiter, vorzustellen. Sie kommt aus München in Deutschland, um unsere schöne Stadt, Chicago, kennenzulernen. Hier ist meine Kusine Jutta!

2.2

JUTTA HEITER: Danke, Otto. Es freut mich sehr hier zu sein.

OTTO WETAR: Jutta, wie ist das Wetter heute in Deutschland?

JUTTA HEITER: Ach, das Wetter ist jetzt wirklich schrecklich. Es regnet überall.

OTTO WETAR: Ja, dann hast du viel Glück hier zu sein. *(Consults papers)* Heute gibt es Wolken* in Chicago und viel Wind. Aber jetzt beginnt unser Programm. Wohin gehen wir heute?

JUTTA HEITER: Hmm. . . Lass uns sehen wie das Wetter in Capri in Italien ist.

OTTO WETAR: Capri, Italien! Ausgezeichnet! *(Puts on earphones)* Wir werden mit unserer Korrespondentin, Tara Braun, in Capri sprechen. Tara, bist du dort? Kannst du mich hören?

TARA BRAUN *(Lying on beach, is applying sun lotion, microphone between knees)*

OTTO WETAR: Tara! Bist du dort? Hörst du mich? Tara Braun!

TARA BRAUN *(Suddenly grabs mike, removes sunglasses, gets professional)*: Hallo, Otto! Wie geht's? Wie ist das Wetter heute in Chicago?

OTTO WETAR: Es gibt Wolken und viel Wind. Wie ist das Wetter in Capri?

TARA BRAUN: Ach, hier ist die Situation sehr ernst.* Es ist heiss. Es ist sehr heiss. Otto, viele Leute sind hier mit mir am Strand.* Die Leute haben keine Energie, weil es so heiss ist.

JUTTA HEITER *(Puts on her earphones)*: Die Armen.

OTTO WETAR: Das ist furchtbar!* Was machen die Leute wenn es so heiss ist, Tara?

TARA BRAUN: Sie leiden* sehr viel! Sie sind ja sehr durstig.* Sie trinken viel Wasser und Zitronenlimonaden.

JUTTA HEITER: Gibt es auch Sonne?

TARA BLAU: Ach ja! Es gibt viel, viel Sonne. Es ist eine sehr ernste Situation.

JUTTA HEITER: Das tut mir sehr leid.

TARA BRAUN: Ja, und da gibt' s noch etwas.

OTTO WETAR: Erzähl uns, Tara, was los ist.

TARA BRAUN: Mit so viel Hitze* und so viel Sonne, brauchen die Leute sehr wenig Kleidung. Könnt ihr euch vorstellen!* So eine Schande!*

OTTO WETAR *(Wistfully)*: Ja, Tara, ich kann mir das vorstellen.

TARA BRAUN: Die Mädchen tragen nur kleine "Bikinis."

OTTO WETAR: Ach, das ist ja schrecklich!* Tara, kann ich dir irgendwie helfen? Ich fahre sofort zum Flughafen.

JUTTA HEITER *(Scandalized)*: Otto!

2.3

TARA BRAUN: Nein, nein, nein, Otto. Dafür bin ich verantwortlich.* Danke vielmals. Heute werde ich mich amüsieren, ich meine, in der Sonne **leiden,** so wie die andern Leute. Ich bin Tara Braun, mit meinem Bericht• aus Capri in Italien. Tschüs!

OTTO WETAR *(Sighing):* Jetzt kehren wir zurück zum Kanal PAN-ORAMA in Chicago, ihr Lieblingskanal, der Kanal, der Ihnen täglich Europas Wetter berichtet. Ich heisse Otto Wetar und hier ist meine Kusine, Jutta.

JUTTA HEITER: Otto, wie ist das Wetter jetzt in Chicago?

OTTO WETAR: Sehen wir mal. *(Reads report)* Heute ist es windig, und wir haben Wolken.

JUTTA HEITER *(After a pause, brightly):* Wohin fahren wir jetzt, Otto?

OTTO WETAR: Wir fahren in die Schweiz, nach Zermatt, wo das Matterhorn* liegt.

JUTTA HEITER: Fantastisch!

OTTO WETAR: Wir sprechen mit Jürgen Hoch, unserem Schweizer Korrespondenten am Matternhorn, der auch ein guter Freund ist. Jürgen! Bist du da?

JÜRGEN HOCH *(Sitting inside a restaurant, stuffing himself with food and drink, microphone lies on table)*

OTTO WETAR: Jürgen! Jürgen Hoch! Hörst du mich?

JÜRGEN HOCH *(Grabs mike, wipes mouth, becomes professional):* Otto Wetar? Mein guter Freund! Wie geht's? Wie ist das Wetter heute in Chicago?

OTTO WETAR: Es gibt Wind und Wolken — wie immer. Wie ist das Wetter dort bei dir?

JÜRGEN HOCH: Ach, es ist furchtbar! Es ist kalt. Es ist sehr, sehr kalt. Und es schneit. Ich bin hier in den Bergen, *(Peers out imaginary window)* und ja, es schneit immer noch. *(Takes big bite of food)*

OTTO WETAR: Ja, wo bist du denn? Bist du in einem Restaurant?

JÜRGEN HOCH: Ja, Otto. Wenn es so kalt draussen ist, bleibe ich im Restaurant. Ich esse gerade Mittagessen hier in Zermatt, weil es so kalt draussen ist.

JUTTA HEITER: Meinst du denn, dass das Wetter schlecht ist? Gibt es vielleicht ein Gewitter?

JÜRGEN HOCH: Eigentlich, nicht. Es ist sehr schön draussen. Es gibt Sonne, aber es ist sehr kalt. Es ist doch furchtbar! *(Takes another bite of food)*

JUTTA HEITER: Warum ist es furchtbar, Jürgen?

JÜRGEN HOCH: Na, ja, die Leute leiden sehr viel. Sie kommen ins Restaurant nach dem Schilaufen. Es ist ihnen sehr kalt, und ihre Gesichter sind sehr rot. Dann müssen sie viele Tassen heisse Schokolade trinken, um sich zu wärmen.

OTTO WETAR: Sagst du, Jürgen, dass die Leute schilaufen?

JÜRGEN HOCH: Natürlich. Es ist sehr schwer im Schnee zu laufen; deshalb laufen die Leute Schi, wenn sie vom Berg herunter kommen. Nicht nur die Männer, Otto, sondern auch die Frauen und die Kinder.

OTTO WETAR: Läufst du auch Schi, Jürgen?

JÜRGEN HOCH: Ach, nein. Ich arbeite. Mein Tisch ist am Fenster. Wenn das Wetter sich ändert, sehe ich es sofort. Jetzt ist übrigens Zeit für die Nachspeise. Ich bin Jürgen Hoch, und ich berichte direkt aus Zermatt in der Schweiz.

OTTO WETAR *(Depressed)*: Jetzt kehren wir zurück zum Kanal PAN-ORAMA, ihr Lieblingskanal, der Kanal, der Ihnen täglich Europas Wetter berichtet.

JUTTA HEITER: Otto, wie ist das Wetter in Chicago jetzt?

OTTO WETAR: Sehen wir mal. *(Reads report dully)* Wir haben noch immer Wind und Wolken, aber jetzt regnet es auch.

JUTTA HEITER *(Pauses, sighs)*: Wohin gehen wir jetzt, Otto?

OTTO WETAR *(Sourly):* Es ist mir nicht wichtig*.

JUTTA HEITER *(Brightly):* Besuchen wir einen Park in Wien in Österreich. Vielleicht den schönen Stadtpark!

OTTO WETAR: Also, gut. Sprechen wir mit unserem Korrespondenten, Kurt Grass. Kurt! Bist du dort?

KURT GRASS: *(Lying in the grass, arms behind head, dozing, mike on chest)*

OTTO WETAR: Kurt! Kurt Grass! Hörst du mich? Bist du da?

KURT GRASS *(Sits up suddenly, grabs mike, becomes professional:* Otto Wetar? Hallo! Wie geht's dir? Wie ist das Wetter heute in Chicago?

OTTO WETAR *(Glaring):* Es ist wolkig, es gibt Wind, und es regnet. Warum ist das wichtig? Wie ist das Wetter in Wien in Österreich?

KURT GRASS: Hier ist das Wetter schön. Es ist nicht heiss. Es ist nicht kalt. Es gibt keine Wolken. Aber, es ist furchtbar!

OTTO WETAR: Warum, Kurt?

KURT GRASS: Ich bin im Stadtpark. Viele Familien unterhalten sich gut im Park. Sie machen ein Picknick, sie ruhen sich aus, sie spielen, sie singen. Sie wissen nicht was für eine Gefahr* sie erwartet.

2.5

JUTTA HEITER *(Alarmed)*: Was für eine Gefahr, Kurt? Ein Erdbeben?* Hagel?* Ein Gewitter?*

KURT GRASS: Nein, Jutta. Ameisen.*

JUTTA HEITER: Ameisen!

KURT GRASS *(Grimly)*: Ja, Ameisen. Seit einer halben Stunde, habe ich neun Ameisen auf meinen Beinen und noch fünf auf meinen Armen.

OTTO WETAR *(Dully)*: Ameisen.

KURT GRASS: Ja, Otto. Während du in Chicago bist, hinter deinem Schreibtisch, ich draussen bin, in einer Welt, die gefährlich ist. Aber ich beklage* mich nicht. So ist das Leben eines Korrespondenten. Otto, Jutta, bis nächstes Mal. Ich bin Kurt Grass, direkt aus Wien in Österreich.

OTTO WETAR *(Places suitcase on desk, stuffs it with clothing as he speaks)*: Jetzt kehren wir zurück zu Kanal PAN-ORAMA in Chicago, ihr Lieblingskanal, der Kanal, der Ihnen täglich Europas Wetter berichtet. Ich heisse Otto Wetar und das ist meine Kusine, Jutta Heiter. *(Quickly exits with suitcase)*

JUTTA HEITER *(Pauses, then addresses camera awkwardly)*: Heute gibt es in Chicago Wind, es ist wolkig, und es regnet sehr. *(Stands, grabs her suitcase, and calls)* Otto, warte auf mich. Ich komm mit. Wohin fahren wir? *(Runs after OTTO WETAR, and Exits)*

DAS ENDE

WORTSCHATZ (in order of appearance in the play)

Wolke, die	*cloud*	Matterhorn, das	*Swiss mountain (highest)*
ernst	*serious*	wichtig	*important*
furchtbar	*terrible*	Gefahr, die	*danger*
leiden	*to suffer*	Erdbeben. das	*earthquake*
durstig	*thirsty*	Hagel, der	*hail*
erzählen	*to tell (story)*	Gewitter, das	*storm*
Hitze, die	*heat*	Ameise, die	*ant*
vorstellen, sich	*to imagine*	beklagen, sich	*to complain*
Schande, die	*shame*		
schrecklich	*terrible*		
verantwortlich	*responsible*		

3. Das Verlorene Buch
✖ Overview ✖

SYNOPSIS: Georg searches his house in vain for his missing library book as his family waits impatiently to leave for the library.

> LANGUAGE OBJECTIVES:
> Vocabulary: objects and furniture in the home
> Structures: auxiliary verbs, prepositions

PRODUCTION NOTES:

The classroom "stage" should resemble a living room as closely as possible. Chairs may be draped with comforters and cushions to look like sofas as well as armchairs. Ask students to bring fabric to hang for curtains and common livingroom furnishings such as a throw rug, a vase, a potted plant, and so on to complete a comfortable livingroom area.

TO EXTEND THE PLAY'S LENGTH:

Add more places for Georg to search for his book. Add more ridiculous objects for him to find instead of his book.

Add a father napping on the living room sofa, who always groggily wants to know what Georg is doing all around the living room.

TO REDUCE THE PLAY'S LENGTH:

Reduce the number of places Georg looks for his book.

Delete the kitchen section and instead have Georg ultimately find his book in the living room.

STAGING SUGGESTION:

3. Das Verlorene Buch

CHARACTERS: 4 Actors
    MUTTER
    GEORG (a twelve year old boy)
    OSKAR (his older brother)
    ILSE (his older sister)

SETTING: a comfortable living room: contains a sofa, an armchair, drapes, a coffee table, a television set, a rug (any size, situated under the armchair)

PROPS: MUTTER, OSKAR and ILSE each need to hold a pile of books. To be placed in living room prior to play and according to script: a mechanical pencil, a hairbrush, a piece of chocolate cake, 2 toy cars, some loose change, shoes, socks, a TV remote control, a photo, a tiny key.
Off-stage: a purse, a large colorful book on insects

AT RISE: *OSKAR and ILSE stand in the living room, each holding a pile of books:*

ILSE *(Calling to MUTTER who is off stage):* Mutti, Oskar und ich müssen zur Bibliothek gehen. Sie schliesst in einer Stunde.

OSKAR: Mutti, ich muss ein paar Bücher zurückbringen.

ILSE: Und ich muss ein Buch über berühmte* Forscher* suchen. Ich brauch es für ein Projekt in Geschichte.

MUTTER *(Enters with a pile of books in her arms):* Ja, ich muss auch zur Bibliothek fahren. Ich muss diese Bücher heute zurückbringen. Wo ist denn euer Bruder?

OSKAR: Georg, wo bist du?

GEORG *(From off stage):* Ich bin im Schlafzimmer.

OSKAR: Was machst du in deinem Schlafzimmer?

GEORG: Nichts — ich höre Musik.

MUTTER: Na, komm doch. Dein Bruder, deine Schwester und ich fahren jetzt zur Bibliothek.

3.2

GEORG *(From off stage)*: Ich will nicht zur Bibliothek mitfahren. Ich will Musik im Radio hören.

MUTTER: Es tut mir leid, aber wir müssen trotzdem zur Bibliothek fahren. Wir müssen unsere Bücher heute zurückbringen. Bring deine Bücher mit.

OSKAR: Beeil dich! Die Bibliothek wird bald schliessen.

GEORG *(Enters, trudging in unhappily and sighing mightily)*: Ich hab' nur **ein** Bibliotheksbuch. Es ist hier im Wohnzimmer.

MUTTER: Also, bring es her. Es ist schon spät. Wir müssen uns beeilen.

GEORG *(Looks around)*: Wo ist mein Buch?

OSKAR: Ach, du Dummkopf. Wie sollen wir das wissen? Wie heisst denn dein Buch?

GEORG: Mmmm . . . ich glaube es heisst: Die Fantastische Welt der Insekten.

MUTTER: Also bitte, Georg, schau mal, ob dein Buch auf dem Tisch ist.

GEORG *(Looking through pile of books on the table)*: Da gibt es viele Bücher auf dem Tisch, aber mein Insektenbuch ist nicht da.

MUTTER: Such es dann **unter** dem Tisch.

GEORG *(Looks under the table, then answers)*: Nein, mein Insektenbuch ist nicht unter dem Tisch, aber schau her! Hier ist ein sehr schöner mechanischer Bleistift *(Starts to play with it)*.

OSKAR: Das ist mein Bleistift, und er ist neu! Gib ihn her! *(Grabs it away from him)*!

MUTTER: Such dann dein Buch **auf** dem Sofa.

GEORG *(Looks on sofa)*: Nein, mein Buch ist nicht auf dem Sofa, aber, schau her. Hier ist eine lila Bürste *(Starts to brush his hair)*!

ILSE: Georg, das ist meine Bürste! Dein Haar ist schmutzig. Du darfst meine Bürste nicht benützen. Gib sie mir! *(She grabs it away from him)*

MUTTER: Vielleicht ist dein Buch **zwischen** den Polstern.* Heb die Polster auf and such dein Buch dort drinnen.

GEORG *(Looks between and under the cushions)*: Nein, ich sehe mein Insektenbuch nicht, aber, schau mal! Hier sind drei Kekse* . . . und 49 Pfennig . . . 2 kleine Autos . . . und, ein Foto von Mutti in ihrem Badeanzug am Strand!

MUTTER: Georg, gib mir dieses Foto! *(She grabs it away from him, he starts to bite into one of the cookies)*

ILSE: Georg, was machst du jetzt?

GEORG: Ich werde die Kekse essen.

ILSE: Diese Kekse sind zu alt. Die Bibliothek wird schon in 40 Minuten schliessen. Bitte, such dein Buch weiter!

GEORG: Na ja, wo ist denn mein Buch?

MUTTER: Ich weiss nicht, Georg. Such es auf dem Teppich, **neben** dem Sessel.

GEORG *(Crawls on rug around armchair):* Nein, mein Insektenbuch ist nicht auf dem Teppich neben dem Sessel, aber, schau mal! Hier ist eine Illustrierte und die Kontrolle für den Fernseher.

OSKAR: Wunderbar! Die verlorene Kontrolle! Jetzt kann ich das Fussballspiel ansehen! *(Takes the remote control, sprawls in the armchair facing the TV)*

ILSE: Steh auf, Oskar! Wir müssen zur Bibliothek fahren.

OSKAR: Ja, ich weiss das . . . aber Georg hat sein Buch immer noch nicht. Während er es sucht, schau ich mir das Fussballspiel im Fernsehen an.

MUTTER *(Irked):* Stell die Kontrolle neben dem Fernseher. Du siehst dir jetzt das Fussballspiel nicht an. Georg, warum suchst du nicht dein Insektenbuch **beim** Vorhang?

GEORG: Also gut, Mutti . . . ich sehe ein Paar Schuhe beim Vorhang . . . und Ilse's Socken . . . und, schau her! Ein kleiner Schlüssel!

ILSE *(Grabs it away):* Das ist mein Schlüssel. Er ist sehr wichtig. Gib ihn zu mir!

GEORG: Aber mein Insektenbuch ist nicht hier.

MUTTER: Suchst du es **vor** dem Vorhang oder **hinter** dem Vorhang?

GEORG: Ich suche es vor dem Vorhang.

MUTTER: Dann such es hinter dem Vorhang.

GEORG *(Complaining):* Mutti, ich bin müde.

OSKAR: Ich auch. Ich möchte das Fussballspiel ansehen.

MUTTER: Georg, such dein Buch hinter dem Vorhang. Warum passt du nicht auf deine Sachen auf? Die Bibliothekbücher sind deine Verantwortung.

ILSE: Mutti, die Bibliothek schliesst schon in 25 Minuten.

MUTTER: Ja, ich weiss, mein Kind.

GEORG *(Sighing as he looks):* Hinter dem Vorhang . . . da gibt's eine Gabel, eine Brille, ein Stück Torte . . . und eine tote Schabe* . . . aber mein Insektenbuch ist nicht hier. Ilse, willst du das Stück Torte essen?

ILSE *(Turns away in disgust):* Ach, du bist ekelhaft!*

MUTTER: Georg! Jetzt spreche ich dich im Ernst.* Finde dein Buch sofort!*

ILSE: Die Bibliothek schliesst in 20 Minuten!

3.4

GEORG: Ich weiss nicht mehr wo ich suchen soll. Mein Insektenbuch ist nicht da.

MUTTER: Ich weiss auch nicht mehr. Es ist nicht **auf** oder **unter** dem Sofa. Es ist nicht **zwischen** den Polstern des Sofas. Es ist nicht **vor** oder **hinter** dem Vorhang. Es ist nicht **auf** dem Teppich **neben** dem Sessel.

ILSE: Mutti, die Bibliothek schliesst schon in 15 Minuten.

MUTTER: Georg, wir müssen zur Bibliotek ohne dein Buch fahren. Ich bin sehr böse auf dich. Bitte, bring mir die Schlüssel fürs Auto.

GEORG: Wo sind die Schlüssel für das Auto?

MUTTER: Georg, sie sind in meiner Handtasche, wie immer.

GEORG: Und wo ist deine Handtasche, Mutti?

MUTTER: Meine Handtasche ist natürlich in der Küche, auf dem Telefonbuch.

GEORG *(Exits briefly, then returns, holding purse, keys and insect book! Speaks smugly to MUTTER)*: Ja, Mutti. Die Schlüssel sind in deiner Handtasche, auf dem Telefonbuch, und das Telefonbuch ist — **auf meinem Buch, <u>Die Fantastische Welt der Insekten.</u>**

ILSE: Fantastisch! Die Bibliothek wird in 15 Minuten schliessen. Gehen wir jetzt schnell! *(All EXIT)*

DAS ENDE

WORTSCHATZ (in order of appearance in the play)

berühmt	*famous*
Forscher, der	*explorer*
Polster, der	*pillow*
Kekse, die *(pl)*	*cookies*
Schabe, die	*cockroach*
ekelhaft	*nasty*
im Ernst	*seriously*
sofort	*immediately*

4. Marlene
❊ Overview ❊

SYNOPSIS: Two simple-minded young men meet a beautiful stranger in the park. They try to coax her into conversation, but she only talks about her car in rapturous, mechanical phrases.

LANGUAGE OBJECTIVES:
Vocabulary: nature
Structures: present tense verb conjugations

PRODUCTION NOTES:
  Marlene's role is not demanding linguistically, as she only repeats one stock phrase throughout the play. She does, however, have a challenging dramatic role as an animatronic robot, who is so lifelike that she fools the two dim-witted young men who chance upon her in the park. Marlene must say her line exactly the same way every time and must never change position on the park bench.
  IMPORTANT! Any time anything touches either of Marlene's arms, her voice mechanism is activated.

TO EXTEND THE PLAY'S LENGTH:
  Add to Max and Franz's dialogue: they may try to discuss the weather, sports, cars, movies and so on with Marlene.

TO REDUCE THE PLAY'S LENGTH:
  Omit Max and Franz's dialogue regarding their jobs and talents.

STAGING SUGGESTION:

4. *Marlene*

CHARACTERS: 5 Actors, 1 Crew Member
    MARLENE (a beautiful animatronic lady, kind of like a talking mannequin
    ERNST (an auto show employee)
    HOLGER (an auto show employee, colleague of ERNST)
    MAX (a dim-witted pretentious young man)
    FRANZ (a dim-witted pretentious young man, MAX's buddy)
    Also needed: a crew member in charge of dropping pinecones on MARLENE's arm, as specified in script

SETTING: A bench in a park. Tall potted plants and hanging baskets to create the illusion of trees and gardens in the classroom or stage. Students may paint an optional backdrop of a park scene on butcher paper or a white sheet.

PROPS: Two pine cones

AT RISE: *ERNST and HOLGER are carefully arranging a lovely mannequin, MARLENE, on a park bench.*

ERNST *(Worriedly, to HOLGER):* Glaubst du dass wir sie hier lassen können?
HOLGER: Natürlich! Wir bleiben ja nur eine halbe Stunde weg. *(Looks around)* Niemand* ist hier im Park. Niemand kommt. Gehen wir jetzt! Ich bin müde. Ich brauche einen Kaffee.
ERNST *(Doubtful):* Ich weiss nicht. Ich will auch einen Kaffee, aber wir sind für Marlene verantwortlich. Was machen wir wenn ihr etwas passiert? Holger, ich bleibe lieber hier mit ihr. Ich habe Angst, sie allein zu lassen.
(Pats Marlene's arm)

4.2

MARLENE *(In a rapturous, beguiling, mechanical voice):* Komm mit mir! Zusammen entdecken wir die Autobahnen und Strassen in meinem neuen Luxuswagen!

HOLGER *(Ignoring MARLENE's voice):* Hör mal, Ernst. Marlene ist ja kein Mensch. Du vergisst, dass Marlene nur eine Maschine ist. Sie ist eine Schaufensterpuppe.* Wir brauchen sie, um neue Autos zu verkaufen. Verstehst du? Sie spricht, wenn man ihren Arm berührt. Schau mal, Ernst. *(Shakes Marlene's hand vigorously and talks to her)* Fräulein, Entschuldigung, Sie haben eine Schabe* im Haar.

MARLENE *(Always in an identical voice):* Komm mit mir! Zusammen entdecken wir die Autobahnen und Strassen in meinem neuen Luxuswagen!

HOLGER *(Kneels dramatically in front of MARLENE, grabs her arms):* Marlene, ich liebe dich, ich schätze* dich, ich denke nur an dich! Liebst du mich auch? Sprich, meine Liebe!

MARLENE: Komm mit mir! Zusammen entdecken wir die Autobahnen und Strassen in meinem neuen Luxuswagen!

HOLGER: Siehst du, Ernst? Marlene ist eine Maschine. Sie ist ein Roboter. Gehen wir jetzt. Es gibt ein Restaurant in der Nähe.

ERNST: Wann kommen wir dann zurück?

HOLGER: Wir kommen in einer halben Stunde zurück. Du hast mein Wort.

ERNST *(Tenderly places MARLENE's arms in a natural position, arranges the position of her face as if to gaze at tree branches, then exits with HOLGER)*

MARLENE *(Alone on set):* Komm mit mir! Zusammen entdecken wir die Autobahnen und Strassen in meinem neuen Luxuswagen! *(Fifteen seconds pass, nothing happens. A pinecone falls on MARLENE's arm, activating her voice mechanism.)*

MARLENE: Komm mit mir! Zusammen entdecken wir die Autobahnen und Strassen in meinem neuen Luxuswagen!

(MAX and FRANZ enter and stop short when they spy MARLENE on bench)

MAX *(Nudges FRANZ with elbow):* Guck mal, Moritz! Ein Fräulein!

FRANZ: Wo?

MAX: Dort drüben. Sie sitzt auf der Bank.

FRANZ: Ja, ich sehe sie schon. Sie ist sehr hübsch!* *(Stares for a moment)* Was tut das Mädchen?

MAX: Ich weiss nicht. Vielleicht lernt sie, aber sie hat keine Bücher... Vielleicht studiert sie die Natur...

FRANZ: Welche Natur?

MAX: Die Natur im Park, Dummkopf. Die Bäume, die Blumen, die Vögel... ich möchte dieses schöne Mädchen gern kennenlernen. *(Starts to approach her, FRANZ grabs him)*

FRANZ: Nein, Max! Dieses Mädchen ist sehr schön. Wahrscheinlich erwartet sie einen Freund.

MAX: Das macht nichts. Gehen wir hin! Wir können sie begrüssen.

(MAX and FRANZ tuck in their shirts, adjust their pants and smooth back their hair in a pretentious manner, then swagger over to MARLENE. MARLENE, of course, does not acknowledge their approach.)

MAX *(Gallantly)*: Guten Tag, Fräulein. Ich heisse MAX and mein Freund heisst FRANZ. *(Pauses for her response, then continues)* Wie heissen Sie?

FRANZ *(Proudly)*: Wir beide arbeiten in einem Videogeschäft.

MAX *(With boorish pride)*: Aber ich arbeite nicht montags, weil ich Karate lerne. *(Demonstrates karate move)*

FRANZ *(Trying to outdo MAX)*: Und ich arbeite dienstags nicht weil ich mit einer Schwimmmannschaft schwimme. *(Awkward pause)* Mieten Sie Videos? Haben Sie Filme gern? *(Whispers to MAX)* Diese Frau spricht nicht viel.

MAX: *(Sits next to her on bench, casually puts arm on bench behind her)* Fräulein, ich sehe dass es Ihnen gut gefällt, die Natur anzusehen. Die Bäume sind sehr schön, nicht war? Eine Familie von Eichhörnchen* wohnt in diesem Baum. Mein Freund und ich gehen jeden Tag hier spazieren. Wir bewundern die Bäume, wir hören den Vögeln zu— Entschuldigung, Fräulein, eine Mücke* beisst Ihren Arm! *(He slaps imaginary mosquito away, activating her speech)*

MARLENE: Komm mit mir! Zusammen entdecken wir die Autobahnen und Strassen in meinem neuen Luxuswagen!

MAX *(Startled, moves away)*: Was sagen Sie? *(Looks at FRANZ, who shrugs shoulders baffled)* Fräulein, fühlen Sie sich wohl? *(Touches her arm gently)* Fräulein?

MARLENE: Komm mit mir! Zusammen entdecken wir die Autobahnen und Strassen in meinem neuen Luxuswagen!

4.4

MAX *(Lamely)*: Haben Sie denn ein neues Automobil? *(Another pinecone falls down and hits MARLENE'S arm)*

MARLENE: Komm mit mir! Zusammen entdecken wir die Autobahnen und Strassen in meinem neuen Luxuswagen!

FRANZ *(Nervously because he realizes that something is not quite right with this lady)*: Ich danke Ihnen, Fräulein, aber heute kann ich nicht die Autobahnen und Strassen mit Ihnen entdecken, weil ich arbeiten muss. *(Touches her arm)* Sie erinnern sich doch, dass ich in einem Videogeschäft arbeite?

MARLENE: Komm mit mir! Zusammen entdecken wir die Autobahnen und Strassen in meinem neuen Luxuswagen!

FRANZ *(Apprehensively, angrily)*: Fräulein, Sie haben ein Problem! Ich weiss nicht, was mit Ihnen los ist, aber ich will nicht die Welt mit Ihnen entdecken! *(Touches her arm for emphasis)* Auch will ich nicht den Park oder die Strassen mit Ihnen entdecken.

MARLENE: Komm mit mir! Zusammen entdecken wir die Autobahnen und Strassen in meinem neuen Luxuswagen!

FRANZ *(Exasperated, squats in front of her, grabs both her elbows)*: Sie sollen lieber ein Krankenhaus* entdecken!

MARLENE: Komm mit mir! Zusammen entdecken wir die Autobahnen und Strassen in meinem neuen Luxuswagen!

(At this moment, ERNST and HOLGER enter: Run to MARLENE with concern when they see MAX and FRANZ bothering her)

ERNST: Marlene, ist alles gut mit dir?

HOLGER: Wenn alles nicht gut mit Marlene ist, sprechen wir mit der Polizei.

(MAX and FRANZ step back and watch as ERNST and HOLGER carefully examine MARLENE's arms, neck and head)

ERNST *(Sighs with relief)*: Du kannst dich beruhigen,* Holger. Gott sei Dank, ist alles gut mit Marlene. Wir werden sie niemals mehr allein im Park lassen.

FRANZ *(Amazed)*: Dieses seltsame* Mädchen hat **zwei** Freunde? *(To ERNST and HOLGER)* Ihr seid verrückt! Und diese Frau ist auch verrückt. She spricht nur über Autobahnen und Luxusautos.

MAX: **Ihr** könnt die wilden Strassen zusammen entdecken. Gehen wir schon, Franz! *(MAX and FRANZ exit)*

23

4.5

HOLGER: Das sind wirklich seltsame Männer! Ernst, fasss den Arm der Schaufensterpuppe an. Sehen wir ob sie noch spricht *(ERNST touches MARLENE's arm)*

MARLENE: Komm mit mir! Zusammen entdecken wir die Autobahnen und Strassen in meinem neuen Luxuswagen!

ERNST: Ausgezeichnet! Gott sei dank! Sie spricht noch sehr gut.

HOLGER: Dann gehen wir schon! Die Neue Autoausstellung* beginnt schon in einer Stunde. Lassen wir sie beim Eingang*. Alle Besucher sind immer entzückt wenn sie den Marleneroboter* sehen. *(They lift her from bench and carry or lead her away)*

MARLENE: Komm mit mir! Zusammen entdecken wir die Autobahnen und Strassen in meinem neuen Luxuswagen! *(EXIT all)*

DAS ENDE

WORTSCHATZ (in order of appearance in the play)

niemand	*noone*
Schaufensterpuppe, die	*mannequin*
Schabe, die	*cockroach*
schätzen	*to value, treasure*
hübsch	*pretty*
Eichhörnchen, das	*squirrel*
Mücke, die	*mosquito*
Krankenhaus, das	*hospital*
sich beruhigen	*calm down*
seltsam	*strange, odd*
Autoausstellung, die	*automobile exhibit*
Eingang, der	*entrance*
Marlenenroboter, der	*the Marlene robot*

5. Das Ideale Haustier
❣ Overview ❣

SYNOPSIS: Renate goes to the pet store to buy the perfect animal companion for herself.

LANGUAGE OBJECTIVES:
  Vocabulary: domesticated animals
  Structures: descriptive adjectives

PRODUCTION NOTES:
   The customers who barge into the pet store, interrupting Herr Stolz and Renate should be animated and should really "ham" up their roles. Their roles add the action necessary to keep the play entertaining to the audience. They always burst in just as Herr Stolz is about to name the mystery animal, thereby prolonging the suspense.

TO EXTEND THE PLAY'S LENGTH:
   Create roles for additional colorful characters who mistakenly enter the pet store.
   Add dialogue in which Renate chooses additional traditional pets she wants to buy and for which Herr Stolz finds reasons to discourage her.

TO REDUCE THE PLAY'S LENGTH:
   Omit any "customer" character roles and dialogue.

STAGING SUGGESTION:

5. Das Ideale Haustier

CHARACTERS: 6 Actors
RENATE (a sensible customer, between the ages of 17-24)
HERR STOLZ (pet store owner)
FRAU ALTMAN (a hurried housewife, customer)
HERR BAUER (a laconic farmer, customer)
FRÄULEIN ZITTER (a scatterbrained customer)
HERR UNRAT (a businessman, customer)

SETTING: A pet store: a long counter top with several books on animal care, posters hung of common household pets, several empty cages, a terrarium or aquarium

PROPS: A small cage prepared with shavings, *etc.* for a small animal such as a hamster or an iguana, a cleaning rag, a shopping list

AT RISE: *RENATE, holding her purse, enters a pet store and approaches the counter where HERR STOLZ is wiping out a cage with a rag.*

RENATE: Guten Tag.
HERR STOLZ: Guten Tag, Fräulein. Einen Moment, bitte.
RENATE: Kein Problem. Ich habe Zeit. *(Goes to look at animal posters on wall)*
HERR STOLZ: Gut. Jetzt ist dieser Käfig* sauber. Wie kann ich Ihnen helfen?
RENATE: Ich möchte ein Tier kaufen.
HERR STOLZ: Hier sind Sie in einer Tierhandlung.* Was für ein Tier möchten Sie denn?
RENATE: Ich möchte ein Tier, dass anders* als die Tiere meiner Freunde ist. Ich möchte ein Schweinchen* kaufen.
HERR STOLZ: Ein Schweinchen? Sie haben recht, das ist ein anderes Tier.
RENATE: Ja. Die Schweinchen sind sehr intelligent und sind wirklich sehr saubere Tiere.
HERR STOLZ: Sie haben recht, Fräulein. Sie sind sauber und sie sind intelligent. Aber leider gibt es ein grosses Problem mit Schweinchen.
RENATE: Was ist das Problem?

HERR STOLZ: Das Problem ist, dass es dem Schweinchen immer heiss ist. Man muss sie jeden Tag baden.

RENATE: Dann werde ich kein Schweinchen kaufen. Was für ein Tier empfehlen* Sie mir denn?

HERR STOLZ: Hier habe ich das ideale Haustier für Sie. *(Bends to pick up a small cage or aquarium, sets it gently on the counter)*

RENATE *(Peers into it)*: Was für ein Tier ist das?

FRAU ALTMAN *(Suddenly bursts into store, runs up to counter)*: Mein Herr — ich bin in grosser Eile!* *(Looks at her shopping list)* Ich brauche zwei Kilo Tomaten, ein Pfund Schinken, und einen Liter Milch.

HERR STOLZ *(Huffily)*: Dieses Geschäft ist kein Supermarkt.

FRAU ALTMAN *(Surprised)*: Wirklich nicht?

HERR STOLZ: Nein, Sehen Sie nicht die Käfige? Das ist ein Geschäft für Tiere.

FRAU ALTMAN *(Apologetically)*: Ach, ich muss mich wirklich schämen! Ich suche einen Supermarkt. Meine Familie ist sehr hungrig. Danke. Grüss Gott. *(Exits)*

RENATE: Herr . . .

HERR STOLZ: Stolz, Fräulein.

RENATE: Herr Stolz. wenn ich kein Schweinchen kaufe, dann möchte ich einen Hund.

HERR STOLZ: Einen Hund!

RENATE *(Enthusiastically)*: Ja, Hunde sind sehr freundlich und treu.*

HERR STOLZ: Sie haben recht, Fräulein. Hunde sind sehr freundlich und treu. Aber, leider gibt es ein grosses Problem mit Hunden.

RENATE: Was für ein Problem?

HERR STOLZ: Das Problem ist, dass sie immer hungrig sind. Sie fressen* viel.

RENATE: Das macht mir nichts.

HERR STOLZ: Sie sind auch immer durstig.* Und wenn die grossen Hunde durstig sind, trinken sie gern das Wasser aus der Toilette.*

RENATE: Ach, das ist ekelhaft!* Also, dann werde ich keinen grossen Hund kaufen. Ich kaufe lieber einen kleinen.

HERR STOLZ: Das Problem mit kleinen Hunden ist, dass sie Angst* haben.

RENATE: Das macht nichts. Manchmal hab' ich auch Angst.

HERR STOLZ: Ja, aber wenn ein Hündchen Angst hat, bellt* es. Es bellt viel. Es bellt während der Nacht, wenn Sie müde sind und schlafen wollen.

5.3

RENATE *(Disappointed)*: Na ja, dann will ich keinen Hund kaufen. Welches Tier empfehlen Sie mir?

HERR STOLZ: Ich habe das ideale Haustier für Sie in diesem Käfig. *(Points to aquarium on counter)*

RENATE *(Anxious)*: Welches Tier ist es?

HERR BAUER *(Enters, looks around, ambles over to counter)*: Hallo. Ich will ein grosses, nützliches* Tier kaufen. Ich will eine Kuh kaufen.

HERR STOLZ: Ich verkaufe keine Kühe hier.

HERR BAUER: Ist das nicht ein Geschäft für Tiere?

HERR STOLZ: Ja, aber ich verkaufe keine Kühe. Die Kühe sind auf der Ranch.

HERR BAUER: Dann verkaufen Sie auch keine Pferde?

HERR STOLZ: Nein!

HERR BAUER: Ach, ich habe wirklich kein Glück heute. Danke. Tschüs. *(Exits)*

RENATE: Also gut, Herr Stolz, wenn ich keinen Hund kaufe, dann möchte ich eine Katze kaufen. Katzen sind sehr anmutig*.

HERR STOLZ: Sie haben recht, Fräulein. Die Katzen sind sehr anmutig. Aber *(Sighs)*, leider gibt es ein grosses Problem mit Katzen.

RENATE *(Getting impatient)*: Also, was ist jetzt das Problem? Einer Katze wird es nicht heiss. Sie ist weder hungrig noch durstig, und sie hat keine Angst.

HERR STOLZ: Das Problem mit den Katzen ist, dass sie immer müde sind. Sie wollen immer schlafen. Eine Katze ist nicht sehr interessant.

RENATE: Dann werde ich auch keine Katze kaufen. Was für ein Tier empfehlen Sie mir, Herr Stolz?

HERR STOLZ: Das ideale Haustier für Sie ist in diesem Käfig. *(Points to aquarium on counter)*

RENATE: Welches Tier ist es?

FRÄULEIN ZITTER *(Bursts in, hurries over to counter)*: Ich habe grosse Eile! Zwei Limonaden, bitte.

HERR STOLZ: Fräulein, das ist ein Geschäft für Haustiere. Es ist kein Schnellimbiss.*

FRÄULEIN ZITTER: Ist das wahr? Aber ich bin so durstig! Meine Freundin und ich haben Durst.

HERR STOLZ: Das tut mir sehr leid. Das ist kein Imbiss. Sehen Sie die Käfige?

FRÄULEIN ZITTER: So ein Mist!* Wir sind so durstig. Danke. Tschüs! *(Exits)*

5.4

HERR STOLZ: Ich bekomme schon Kopfschmerzen.

RENATE: Also, Herr Stolz, wenn ich keine Katze kaufe, möchte ich einen Papagei kaufen. Ein Papagei kann sprechen und und ist ein guter Kamerad.*

HERR STOLZ: Sie haben recht, Fräulein. Ein Papagei kann sprechen und ist ein guter Kamerad. Aber leider gibt es ein grosses Problem mit Papageien.

RENATE *(Totally exasperated)*: Was für ein Problem? Einem Papagei wird nicht heiss. Er ist nicht sehr hungrig oder durstig. Er hat keine Angst und ist den ganzen Tag nicht müde.

HERR STOLZ: Das Problem mit Papageien ist, dass es ihnen immer kalt ist. Und wenn einem Papagei kalt ist, wird er die Grippe* bekommen. Wenn ein Papagei die Grippe bekommt, ist es sehr gefährlich für ihn.

RENATE: Dann kaufe ich keinen Papagei. Welches Haustier empfehlen Sie mir?

HERR STOLZ: Das ideale Haustier ist in diesem Käfig.

RENATE: Welches Tier ist es?

HERR STOLZ: Es ist ein—*(He tenderly lifts a rock out of the cage)* gezähmter* Stein.

RENATE *(With disbelief):* Es ist ein **Stein**?

HERR STOLZ: Ein **gezähmter** Stein. Er ist nie hungrig oder durstig. Es ist ihm nicht heiss und nicht kalt. Nie hat er Angst und braucht keinen Schlaf. Nie hat er die Grippe. Ein gezähmter Stein ist das ideale Haustier!

RENATE: Herr Stolz, das ist lächerlich!* Ich werde keinen Stein kaufen. Ein Stein ist kein ideales Haustier.

HERR UNRAT*(Enters store, walks briskly to counter)*: Guten Tag. Meine Tochter ist krank. Sie hat Halsweh!* Ich möchte ihr ein kleines Geschenk kaufen.

HERR STOLZ: Wie alt ist Ihre Tochter?

HERR UNRAT: Sie ist neun Jahre alt.

HERR STOLZ: Wunderbar! Sie haben viel Glück weil ich das ideale Haustier für Ihre Tochter habe! *(Offers rock)*

HERR UNRAT *(Delightedly):* Fantastisch! Das ist ein gezähmter Stein, nicht wahr? Wieviel kostet er?

HERR STOLZ: Der gezähmte Stein und Käfig kosten DM27.

HERR UNRAT: Das ist sehr preiswert.* Sehr gut. *(They exchange money and goods, Herr Unrat exits happily)*

RENATE *(Sighs, resigned):* Also gut. Ich will auch einen Stein kaufen.

HERR STOLZ: Einen **gezähmten** Stein?

RENATE *(Peevishly)*: Ja, einen gezähmten Stein.

HERR STOLZ: Ach, das tut mir sehr leid, Fräulein! Die gezähmten Steine sind sehr beliebt. Sie sind jetzt ausverkauft.* Was für ein anderes Haustier möchten Sie?

DAS ENDE

WORTSCHATZ (In order of appearance in the story)

Käfig, der	*the cage*
Tierhandlung, die	*the pet store*
anders	*unusual, different*
Schweinchen, das	*little pig, piglet*
empfehlen	*to recommend*
Eile, die	*hurry*
treu	*loyal*
durstig	*thirsty*
nützlich	*useful*
Kommode, die	*toilet*
ekelhaft	*nasty*
Angst haben	*to be afraid*
bellen	*to bark*
anmutig	*charming*
Schnellimbiss, der	*snackbar*
So ein Mist!	*What a shame!*
Kamerad, der	*companion*
Grippe, die	*flu*
gezähmt	*domesticated*
lächerlich	*ridiculous*
Halsweh, das	*sore throat*
preiswert	*reasonable price*
ausverkauft	*sold out*

6. Die Geburtstagsfeier
✉ Overview ✉

SYNOPSIS: Max tries valiantly against all odds to attend Frieda's 16th birthday party but he arrives too late . . . or is it too early?

LANGUAGE OBJECTIVES:
  Vocabulary: time expressions, transportation
  Structures: separable prefix verbs

PRODUCTION NOTES:
  Max has a very demanding role with a lot of dialogue and action. The other five roles each have approximately the same number of speaking lines and basically exist in order to interrupt and annoy Max.
  A backdrop of a downtown city street and buildings may be painted on butcher paper or a white sheet. Street signs, bus stop signs and so on may be added to the set.
  Max must carry his gift at all times.

TO EXTEND THE PLAY'S LENGTH:
  Ways to further detain Max: 1) He loses the present and must search for it. 2) He meets friends and they insist he join them for a soda. 3) He takes a taxi and the taxi driver takes him to the airport by mistake.

TO REDUCE THE PLAY'S LENGTH:
  Omit the role of Fräulein Helm.

6. Die Geburtstagsfeier

CHARACTERS: 6 Actors
   MAX (a middle or high school student)
   TONI (a city bus driver)
   FRAU BLUM (a bystander)
   FRÄULEIN HELM (a shopper)
   POLIZIST
   FRIEDA (the birthday girl)

SETTING: None; this is a purely imaginary downtown area

PROPS: Two watches (for MAX and the POLIZIST), an invitation, a gift-wrapped present which contains a hand mirror, a student-generated cardboard bus (approximately 6'x4' with cut-out windows), a paper shopping bag full of purchases, a sign indicating a hospital, a policeman's whistle, a woman's purse

AT RISE: *MAX enters, holding a beautifully gift-wrapped present. He pulls an invitation out of his pocket and silently scans it.*

MAX *talking to himself and to the audience):* Heute hat meine beste Freundin, Frieda, ihren sechzehnten Geburtstag und sie hat mich zu der Geburtsags= feier eingeladen. Das ist ein wichtiger Tag für sie und ich darf nicht spät ankommen. Wie spät ist es? *(Looks at his watch)* Es ist halb zwei, nachmittags (1:30 p.m.). Die Geburtstagsfeier beginnt um halb drei (2:30). Es ist eine Überraschung.* Ich muss mich beeilen. Ich werde ein Taxi rufen, damit ich pünktlich ankommen kann. *(Stands at imaginary street curb and calls for taxi)* Taxi! Taxi! *(Waits impatiently)* Wo sind die Taxis?

FRAU BLUM *(Enters, approaches):* Entschuldigung. Suchen Sie ein Taxi?

MAX: Ja, ich brauche ein Taxi.

FRAU BLUM: Hier halten die Taxis nicht an. Es gibt keine Taxis auf dieser Strasse.

6.2

MAX: Meine liebe Frau, es sind schon zwanzig Minuten vor zwei, und ich muss bei meiner Freundin genau im halb drei sein. Wie komme ich schnell an den Suttnerplatz?

FRAU BLUM: Sie können mit dem Autobus fahren. Nummer 37. Hier kommt einer.

MAX: Fantastisch! Danke vielmals. *(Waits for bus to approach)* Autobus! *(Bus doors open)* Fahren Sie zum Suttnerplatz?

TONI: Ja, dieser Autobus fährt zum Suttnerplatz. Aber zuerst muss ich an der Universität und am Markplatz anhalten.

MAX: Wann hält der Autobus am Suttnerplatz an?

TONI: Wir kommen um zwei Uhr zur Universität. um viertel nach zwei (2:15) zum Markplatz, und um halb drei (2:30) zum Suttnerplatz.

MAX: Wunderbar! *(He boards the bus and sits down, looks at watch)* Jetzt ist es viertel vor zwei (1:45). *(They bounce along for a while)*

TONI *(Comes to a stop):* Universität!

MAX *(Looks at his watch approvingly):* Es ist jetzt zwei Uhr. *(The bus takes off again)*

TONI *(Comes to a stop):* Marktplatz!

MAX *(Nods contentedly to himself again):* Es ist viertel nach zwei nachmittags (2:15). Sehr gut. *(The bus takes off again)* Da komm' ich um halb drei (2:30) bei Frieda an und kann sie gut überraschen. *(The bus suddenly jerks to a stop)*

TONI: Oh, oh, wir haben eine Panne!*

MAX: Was ist los?

TONI: Ich weiss nicht — vielleicht hat es etwas mit dem Getriebe* zu tun. *(Scratches face, thinking)* Der Bus läuft nicht mehr. Sie müssen aussteigen.

MAX *(Panicking):* Aber es ist schon zwei Uhr zwanzig (2:20). Die Geburtstags= feier meiner Freundin beginnt um halb drei (2:30)! Was soll ich machen?

TONI: Es tut mir sehr leid. Sie können laufen.

MAX: Wo ist denn der Suttnerplatz?

TONI *(Trying to be helpful):* Von hier aus, ist er am Ende der *Hauptstrasse, mehr oder weniger zwei Kilometer von hier, rechts.

MAX: Zwei Kilometer?

TONI: Ja, zwei - oder vielleicht drei. Viel Glück! Tschüs!

6.3

MAX *(Starts walking, talking to himself)*: Ach, ich habe wirklich Pech.* Ich will doch Frieda zu ihrem Geburtstag überraschen. Ich bin ihr bester Freund. Und jetzt ist es schon halb drei (2:30)— und hier bin ich, mitten in der Stadt.

FRÄULEIN HELM *(Enters with large shopping bag, trips and falls, items spill out)*: Ach, mein Knöchel!* *(Groans and holds her ankle)*

MAX: Fräulein, was ist Ihnen passiert? Tut Ihnen etwas weh? *(Kneels to help her)*

FRÄULEIN HELM *(Rocks back and forth in pain)*: Mein Knöchel tut mir sehr weh.

MAX: Wie kann ich Ihnen helfen?

FRÄULEIN HELM *(In terrible pain)*: Ich muss ins Krankenhaus. Ich kann nicht laufen. Ach, mein Knöchel tut mir so weh!

MAX: Gibt es ein Krankenhaus in der Nähe?

FRÄULEIN HELM: Ja, es gibt eins in der Nähe — zwei Strassen links. Ich bin Krankenschwester* in diesem Krankenhaus.

MAX *(Looks fretfully at his watch and sighs)*: Ich kann Ihnen helfen zu Fuss gehen.

FRÄULEIN HELM: Danke vielmals. Aber meine Einkäufe — ach, mein Knöchel!

MAX *(Gathers her items, puts them in her shopping bag)*: Ich trage Ihre Tasche. *(He supports her, walks her to imaginary hospital, leaves her, then continues on his way)* Wie spät ist es denn jetzt? *(Looks at watch)* Es ist zwanzig Minuten vor vier (3:40 p.m.) Ach, was soll ich tun? Jetzt ist die Geburtstagsfeier fast vorüber. Und hier bin ich, Friedas bester Freund, mitten in der Stadt. Frieda wird sehr böse auf mich sein. Ihre Mutter wird sich auch ärgern. Jetzt muss ich schnell laufen. *(Starts running)*

POLIZIST *(Enters, sees Max running, blows whistle)*: Junger Mann! Halten Sie! Im Name des Gesetzes! *(Max stops running)* Kommen Sie her, mit den Händen auf dem Kopf! *(Max complies, policeman circles him)* Wohin laufen Sie denn?

MAX: Ich laufe zur Geburtstagfeier meiner Freundin.

POLIZIST: Ja, aber warum laufen Sie?

MAX: Weil ich schon sehr spät bin. Die Feier hat um halb drei (2:30) begonnen*— und jetzt ist es schon vier Uhr zwanzig (4:20)!

POLIZIST: Ja, Sie haben recht. Es ist schon sehr spät für Sie. Was haben Sie denn im Paket?

MAX: Es ist ein Geschenk für meine Freundin.

POLIZIST: Ein Geschenk? Was ist drinnen?

MAX: Ein Silberspiegel.

POLIZIST: Öffnen Sie das Paket bitte.

MAX: Herr Polizist, bitte! Es ist schon spät. Ich hab' keine Zeit mehr.

POLIZIST: Na ja, haben Sie denn Zeit mich auf die Polizeiwache zu begleiten?

MAX *(Unwraps gift, policeman examines mirror).*

POLIZIST: Es ist ein Spiegel.

MAX: Ja.

POLIZIST: Gut, gehen Sie weiter. Amüsieren Sie sich auf der Feier.

MAX *(Running, looks at watch):* Ach! Es ist schon fünf Uhr!

****

FRIEDA *(Enters casually, swinging a purse):* Max, mein Liebchen! Was für eine unerwartete* Überraschung!

MAX: Frieda! *(He looks at her dumbfounded)*

FRIEDA: Was machst du heute in der Stadt? Ich gehe einkaufen. Ich suche neue Schuhe für meinen Geburtstag.

MAX *(Flabbergasted):* Für deinen Geburtstag? *(Looks at watch)* Warum bist du nicht zu Hause? Lässt du deine Geburtstagsgäste allein zu Hause?

FRIEDA *(Laughs):* Du bist ja ein Dummkopf! Schau deine Einladung an. Mein Geburtstag ist in einer Woche! Nächsten Samstag!

DAS ENDE

WORTSCHATZ (in order of appearance in the play)

Überraschung, die	*surprise*
Panne, die	*blowout (tire)*
Getriebe, das	*transmission*
Knöchel, der	*ankle*
Krankenschwester, die	*nurse*
hat . . . begonnen	*has begun*
unerwartet	*unexpected*

7. Arno Verliebt Sich
♥ Overview ♥

SYNOPSIS: Arno tries every way possible to get Anna to notice him, but she is only interested in her book about cats.

> **LANGUAGE OBJECTIVES:**
>   Vocabulary: parts of the body
>   Structures: descriptive adjective agreement

PRODUCTION NOTES:
   IMPORTANT! During any and all of Arno and Leo's dialogue, Anna and Patti should have their heads together quietly discussing pages of their cat book, oblivious to the boys' discussion. Likewise, whenever Arno is at the girls' table, Leo should be engrossed in his food.

TO EXTEND THE LENGTH OF THE PLAY:
   Add more body part-related dialogue. Leo may explain to Arno the ways his appearance differs from current heartthrob movie stars. Arno may expound on Anna's beauty.

TO REDUCE THE LENGTH OF THE PLAY:
   Omit the dialogue about walking confidently with the shoulders thrown back, etc. as well as the dialogue about the clarinet concert.

STAGING SUGGESTION:

7. Arno Verliebt Sich

CHARACTERS: 4 Actors
  ARNO (an insecure middle or high school student, lovestruck over ANNA)
  LEO (ARNO's supportive, but imperturbable friend)
  ANNA (an attractive middle or high school student, very interested in cats)
  Patti (ANNA's friend)

SETTING:
  A school cafeteria containing at least two long tables
  Optional: posters regarding the four food groups and today's lunch menu may be displayed on the walls

PROPS: A large, thick, colorful book on cats, two school cafeteria trays of food which include standard flatware, napkins and the following food: carrots, mashed potatoes, cookies, any kind of meat, and milk cartons

AT RISE: ANNA and PATTI sit together at one table, quietly examining and discussing a book of cats. ANNA has her elbows on the table. ARNO and LEO are seated at a nearby table with their meal trays. LEO is eating his lunch with gusto and ARNO is staring longingly at ANNA

LEO (*Looks with interest at Arno's tray*): Wirst du die Karotten essen?

ARNO (*Dreamily*): Nein, ich habe keinen Hunger.

LEO: Gibst du sie mir?

ARNO: Was sagst du?

LEO: Die Karotten. Die Karotten auf deinem Teller. Was ist denn heute los mit dir?

ARNO: Schau dir das Mädchen dort an. Sie ist sehr hübsch, glaubst du nicht?

LEO (*As he scrapes Arno's carrots on to his tray*): Welches Mädchen? Es gibt viele Mädchen in dieser Cafeteria.

ARNO: Das Mädchen mit dem langen schwarzen Haar, den blauen Augen, und den roten Lippen.

LEO *(Looking around the cafeteria)*: Meinst du das Mädchen, das sich die Nägel* lackiert?*

ARNO: Nein, das Mädchen mit den Ellbogen* auf dem Tisch. Sie und ihre Freundin schauen sich ein Buch an.

LEO: Ja, ich sehe sie jetzt. Stimmt, sie ist wirklich hübsch. Arno, wirst du deine Milch trinken?

ARNO: Ich möchte sie gern kennenlernen. *(Walks over to the girls)* Tag! Ich heisse Arno. Wie heisst ihr? *(Girls look up at him and start giggling; Arno is mystified)* Warum lacht ihr über mich?

ANNA: Du hast Kartoffelbrei* im Gesicht.*

ARNO *(Mortified)*: Ach, entschuldigt mir, bitte! (*(Returns to seat)* Leo, hab' ich Kartoffelbrei im Gesicht?

LEO *(Laughing)*: Ja, schade. Du hast Kartoffelbrei auf deinen Backen* und auch auf deinem Kinn.*

ARNO *(Wipes his face with a napkin)*: Wie sieht mein Gesicht jetzt aus?

LEO: Na ja, es ist so hässlich* wie immer, aber wenigstens ist es sauber.*

ARNO: Gut. *(Returns to girls' table; they are discussing cats, don't notice him)*

PATTI: Ich habe diese Katzen sehr gern, besonders diese mit den geknickten* Ohren and kurzen Schwänzen.*

ANNA: Ja, die sehen ganz anders aus. Manchmal scheint ihr Fell fast blau zu sein.

ARNO: Hallo, noch einmal.

ANNA *(To Patti)*: Das ist der Junge mit dem Kartoffelbrei im Gesicht.

ARNO: Ja, aber jetzt ist mein Gesicht schön sauber. Ich heisse Arno. Wie heisst du?

ANNA: Ich heisse Anna.

ARNO: Es freut mich, dich kennenzulernen. Möchtest du nach der Schule mit mir ins Café gehen?

ANNA: Nein, danke. Ich habe heute keine Zeit.

ARNO: Morgen, vielleicht?

ANNA: Nein, morgen auch nicht. *(Returns attention to the book)* Schau, Patti, wie gefallen dir diese Siamkatzen?

PATTI: Hm... mir gefallen ihre blauen Augen, aber meiner Meinung nach sind die Körper* und Beine* dieser Katzen zu mager.*

7.3

ARNO (*returns dejectedly to his table*): Dieses Mädchen interessiert sich überhaupt nicht für mich. Warum?

LEO: Vielleicht ist sie mehr interessiert an Männern mit Muskeln.*

ARNO: Aber ich habe Muskeln. Schau meine Arme an. Meine Beine sind auch muskulös.

LEO: Arno, bitte, ich will nicht deine Beine bewundern. Kaufst du ein Eis heute?

ARNO: Ich werde ihr die Muskeln meiner Armen und Beinen zeigen. (*Returns to the girls' table*): Hallo, noch einmal. Kommst du mit in die Turnhalle?* (*Flexes his muscles*) Ich gehe jeden Tag hin.

ANNA: Nein, danke.

ARNO: Vielleicht am Samstag?

ANNA: Nein, danke. (*Returns attention to the book*) Hier gibt's einige Fotos von Kätzchen! Sind sie nicht süss?

PATTI: Ja, die sind wirklich süss! Ihre Körper sind so klein, wenn man sie mit ihren grossen Augen, Ohren und Pfoten* vergleicht.*

ARNO (*dejectedly returns to seat*): Meine kräftigen* Arme und Beine interessieren sie nicht.

LEO: Hör mal, Arno. Du musst dich selbstsicher angeben. Steh mit geraden Schultern,* halte deinen Kopf hoch. (*Arno does this*) Sehr gut! Jetzt geh' wieder hin.

ARNO (*returns to girls' table with this "macho" swagger*) Grüss dich, Anna, ich bin wieder da. Möchtest du mit mir spazierengehen? Gehen wir ins Musikzimmer. Ich spiel' dir etwas auf meiner Klarinette vor.

ANNA: Hör mich an, Arno! (*Her voice growing louder and louder*). Ich will nicht mit dir sprechen. Ich will nicht ins Café gehen. Ich will nicht in die Turnhalle gehen. Ich will deine muskulösen Arme und Beine nicht anschauen. Und, endlich, will ich die Musik deiner Klarinette nicht anhören. Ich will nur mit meiner Freundin das Katzenbuch anschauen.

LEO (*hears this, becomes suddenly interested, walks over, talks to Anna*): Ein Katzenbuch? Ich habe Katzen sehr gern. Ich habe eine Katze die Luzi heisst. Ihr sind gerade sieben Kätzchen geboren. Sie ist zu Hause in der Küche. Ihre Augen sind noch zu

PATTI: Ach, ich möchte sie so gern sehen.

7.4

ANNA: Ich auch!

LEO: Vielleicht am Samstag?

ANNA: Können wir sie vielleicht heute schon sehen? Nach der Schule? Geht das? Schau! (*Locks her arm in his, leads him away as Arno watches despondently*) Ich heisse Anna. Und das ist meine Freundin, Patti. Du hast solche muskulösen Arme! Du machst Sport, nicht wahr? Und dein Haar glänzt* so schön! . . . Wie alt sind deine Kätzchen? Darf ich sie streicheln?* (EXIT AND FADE OUT)

DAS ENDE

WORTSCHATZ (in order of appearance in the play)

Nägel, die	*nails*
lackieren	*to polish*
Ellbogen, der	*elbow*
Kartoffelbrei, der	*mashed potatoes*
Gesicht, das	*face*
Backen, die(pl)	*cheeks*
Kinn, das	*chin*
hässlich	*ugly*
sauber	*clean*
geknickt	*doubled over*
Schwanz, der	*tail*
Körper, der	*body*
Bein, das	*leg*
mager	*thin*
Muskeln, die	*muscles*
Turnhalle, die	*gym*
Pfote, die	*paw*
vergleichen	*to compare*
kräftig	*muscular*
Schulter, die	*shoulder*
glänzen	*to glisten*
streicheln	*to pet, stroke*

8. Reisesachen
✂ Overview ✂

SYNOPSIS: Frau Knopf, the clothing store owner, and her employee, Ursula, desperately try to sell their frugal customer, Herr Baum, the amazing One-Fabric-Does-All clothing.

LANGUAGE OBJECTIVES:
   Vocabulary: articles of clothing
   Structures: commands

PRODUCTION NOTES:

This play is pure slapstick. The sillier Herr Baum looks in his "clothing," and the angrier he gets, the better. The salespeople never giggle, but always earnestly tell him how good he looks. Frau Knopf is definitely the dominant personality of the two women. Ursula has very few original thoughts and opinions and always enthusiastically agrees with anything Frau Knopf says.

Herr Baum has an emotional and fairly lengthy monologue toward the end of the play.

TO EXTEND THE LENGTH OF THE PLAY:

Add roles and dialogue for additional customers that enter the store periodically throughout the play. They request items for themselves and other family members, try clothing on, ask how they look, and so on.

TO REDUCE THE LENGTH OF THE PLAY:

Consolidate Frau Baum and Ursula into one role.

STAGING SUGGESTION:

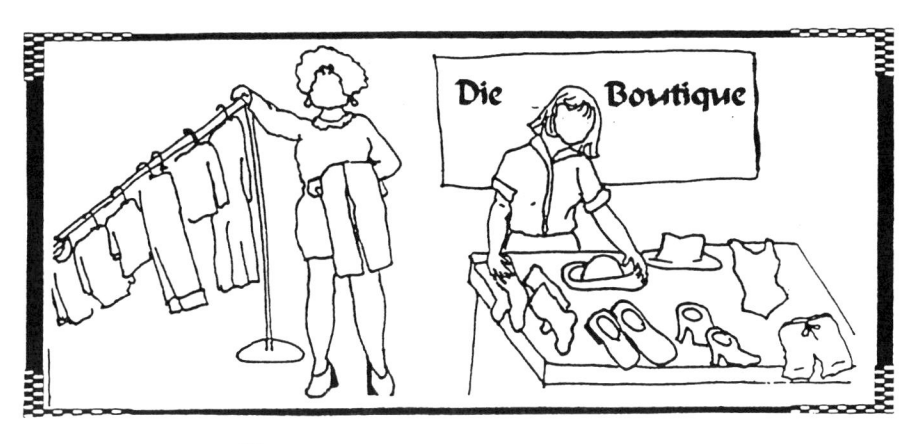

8. *Reisesachen*

CHARACTERS: 3 Actors
    Frau Knopf (the clothing store owner)
    Ursula (an employee)
    Herr Baum (a hapless customer)

SETTING: A clothing store: has a lovely sign on the wall with the name of the store "Die Boutique"
    Furnishings include a rack of clothing on hangers and a counter top displaying shoes, socks, hats, gloves, etc.

PROPS: Hanging on rack: men's slacks, men's dress shirts, men's jackets, also one or more blouses, skirts, and dresses
    Items to be displayed on counter top: hats, shoes, socks, bathing suits, (for men and women), pajamas
    IMPORTANT! Three different cuts of colorful, easy-to-wrap-around fabric: 4-6 yards each (the uglier the better)
    A shopping list, a hand mirror, and (optional) a full-length mirror

AT RISE: *FRAU KNOPF and URSULA are busily arranging clothes on hangers as well as on the counter display. HERR BAUM enters the store and looks through the clothing on racks. Then, as FRAU KNOPF and URSULA watch, he removes a few bills from his wallet, counts them, shakes his head sadly, sighs and prepares to exit. FRAU KNOPF stops him.*

FRAU KNOPF: Guten Tag! Suchen Sie etwas Besonderes? Suchen Sie Hosen oder Schuhe? Oder vielleicht eine Bluse oder einen schönen Rock für Ihre Frau? Oder vielleicht einen Badeanzug für Ihre Tochter?

HERR BAUM *(Dejectly)*: Ich suche alles. Ich brauche viele Sachen.* Ich fahre bald nach Frankreich und brauche viele neue Sachen . . . *(Sighs)* Ich habe eine Liste hier. *(Gets list out of pocket and reads it)* Ich brauche Hemde,

8.2

Hosen, Socken, eine Jacke, einen Badeanzug, einen Pulli, Strümpfe, ein Pyjama, und einen Hut.

FRAU KNOPF: Ursula, zeig bitte dem Herrn die Sachen, die er braucht.

URSULA (*Nods enthusiastically*): Ja, natürlich! (*To HERR BAUM*) Hier in diesem Geschäft haben wir alles, was sie brauchen. (*Shows each item as she names it*). Wir haben Hemden, Pullis, Hosen, und Jacken für Herren. Und hier haben wir Socken, Schuhe, und Badeanzüge. Möchten Sie etwas anprobieren?*

HERR BAUM: Ja . . . mir gefällt alles, was Sie mir zeigen - sie sind ideal für meine Reise, aber . . . nein . . . nein, danke. (*Turns to leave store*)

FRAU KNOPF: Aber, warum, mein Herr? Gibt es ein Problem?

HERR BAUM: Es ist nur — (*opens wallet*) ich habe nicht viel Geld. Also, danke . . . Auf Wiedersehen. (*Turns to leave*)

FRAU KNOPF: Warten Sie nur mal! Unsere Sachen sind nicht teuer.* Ursula, zeig dem Herrn, dass unsere Sachen aus guter Qualität aber auch preiswert* sind.

URSULA (*Nods*): Ja, Frau Knopf. Dieses schöne Kleid kostet nur DM60. Und diese Hose kostet nur DM45. Und dieser schöne Badeanzug kostet nur DM30.

HERR BAUM: Alles ist sehr schön, aber . . . danke, nein, es tut mir leid. Wiedersehen. (*Turns to leave*)

FRAU KNOPF: Wieviel Geld haben Sie mit?

HERR BAUM: Ich habe nur DM30.

FRAU KNOPF (*Thinks frantically, not wanting to lose sale*): Aber, ich verkaufe Ihnen diesen schönen Badeanzug für DM30.

HERR BAUM (*Indignant*): Meine liebe Dame, ich fahre nach Frankreich! Ich brauche viel mehr als einen Badeanzug.

FRAU KNOPF (*Has a sudden brainstorm*): Ursula, bring die "Reisekleidung!"*

URSULA: Ja, Frau Knopf! Die "Reisekleidung!" (*From behind counter, pulls out a long rectangular piece of cloth and hands it to FRAU KNOPF*)

FRAU KNOPF (*Proudly*): Diese Kleidung kostet nur DM30.

HERR BAUM: Welche Kleidung? Ich sehe keine Kleidung.

FRAU KNOPF: Die Kleidung, die ich Ihnen zeige. Die Qualität dieser Kleidung ist ausgezeichnet.* Fassen Sie sie an. Wie weich* sie ist! Sag' es dem Herrn, Ursula.

URSULA: Ja, Frau Knopf. Sehen Sie, mein Herr, wie weich die "Reisekleidung" ist!

8.3

HERR BAUM: Stimmt, aber das ist ja keine Kleidung. Es ist ein Stück Stoff.* Ein Rechteck* aus Stoff.

FRAU KNOPF *(Aghast)*: Aber, mein Herr, Sie wissen gar nichts über die Mode.* Das ist die "Reisekleidung." Sie ist sehr berühmt!* Sehr populär in Frankreich.

HERR BAUM *(Doubtfully)*: Die Reisekleidung? Und sie ist populär in Frankreich?

FRAU KNOPF: Natürlich! Ist das nicht wahr, Ursula?

URSULA *(Nods enthusiastically)*: Ja, Frau Knopf. Sie ist sehr populär in Frankreich.

HERR BAUM: Wie ziehe ich das an?

FRAU KNOPF: Schauen Sie her, Herr — wie heissen Sie?

HERR BAUM: Ich heisse Herr Baum.

FRAU KNOPF: Schauen Sie, Herr Baum, es ist sehr einfach. Ursula, hilf mir bitte. *(FRAU KNOPF wraps the fabric around HERR BAUM's head, turban-style)* Die "Reisekleidung" ist ein Hut. Es ist ein schöner Hut für Sie. Ursula, sieht Herr Baum nicht elegant aus?

URSULA: Ja, Sie haben recht, Frau Knopf. Herr Baum sieht sehr elegant aus. Schauen Sie sich im Spiegel* an *(She offers him a hand mirror)*.

HERR BAUM *(Looks in mirror, then angrily snatches fabric off head)*: Das ist kein Hut. Das ist lächerlich* *(Shows real hat)* Hier ist ein Hut.

FRAU KNOPF *(Gently chiding him)*: Es ist doch ein Hut, Herr Baum, aber es ist möglich, dass er zu gross für Sie ist —

HERR BAUM *Still angry)*: Er ist zu gross für mich!

FRAU KNOPF: Man kann die "Reisekleidung" auch als Hosen verwenden.* Ursula, hilf mir, bitte. *(FRAU KNOPF and URSULA quickly wrap fabric around his lower half to resemble pants)*. Voilá, Herr Baum! Eine neue Hose! In Frankreich werden alle Leute Ihre neuen Hosen bewundern! Sag's ihm, Ursula!

URSULA: Herr Baum, alle Leute in Frankreich werden Ihre neue Hose bewundern. Schauen Sie sie im Spiegel an.

HERR BAUM *(After a look in the mirror, blusters)*: Das ist ja keine Hose! *(He unwraps himself and pulls pants off rack)* Da gibt es Hosen!

FRAU KNOPF *(Musing to Ursula)*: Vielleicht gefällt ihm die Farbe nicht?

URSULA: Das ist möglich, Frau Knopf. Aber die Farbe ist gut für eine Jacke.

FRAU KNOPF: Ursula, was für eine wunderbare Idee. Hilf mir, bitte. *(They wrap him up once again, this time to form a jacket)* Sehen Sie, Herr Baum, die

"Reisekleidung" Farbe spiegelt* die Farbe Ihrer Augen. Wie schön! Findest du nicht, Ursula?

URSULA: Ja, Frau Knopf. Herr Baum ist sehr schick. Besonders seine Augen.

FRAU KNOPF: Wie wunderbar die Reisekleidung ist! Jetzt haben Sie eine Jacke, aber auch *(Rearranges fabric as she chatters)* einen Pullover für den Herbst, und einen Mantel für den Winter!

HERR BAUM: Ich möchte mich im Spiegel ansehen. *(FRAU KNOPF stands purposely in front of the mirror, blocking his view)*

FRAU KNOPF: Herr Baum, Sie brauchen sich nicht ansehen. Die Jacke passt Ihnen sehr gut.

HERR BAUM: Ich möchte mich im Spiegel ansehen. Frau Knopf, bitte! *(She moves out of the way, he looks in mirror)* Das ist lächerlich! Das ist keine Jacke! *(He pulls each item off rack and shakes it angrily as he talks about it)* **Das** ist eine Jacke! Meine Damen, hören Sie zu! **Das** sind Socken—und **das** hier ist ein elender* Stoff. **Hier** ist ein Pyjama —und **das hier** ist wieder ein elender Stoff. Das ist ein Badeanzug—und das hier ist immer noch ein elender Stoff. Das Problem hier ist nicht, ob die Grösse* richtig für mich ist. Das Problem ist einfach, **es gefällt mir nicht**! Und wissen Sie, warum es mir nicht gefällt? Es gefällt mir nicht weil es keine Kleidung ist! Es ist Stoff! *(Dumps fabric in FRAU KNOPF's hands)*

FRAU KNOPF *(Meekly, after a long pause)*: Ist es ein Rock für Ihre Tochter?

HERR BAUM: Es ist kein Rock. Hier ist ein Rock.

FRAU KNOPF: Ist es ein Kleid für Ihre Frau?

HERR BAUM: Es ist kein Kleid. Hier ist ein Kleid. *(Emotionally exhausted)* Hier habe ich DM30. Ich werde diesen Badeanzug kaufen. Das ist alles. Danke. Auf Wiedersehen. *(He hands them the money from his wallet, takes the bathing suit, and EXITS)*

••

FRAU KNOPF: Wie spät ist es?
URSULA *(Looks at her watch)*: Es ist 6:00 Uhr abends.

FRAU KNOPF: Schon 6:00 Uhr? Wunderbar. Schliessen wir das Geschäft! Gehen wir essen! *(She exits but returns immediately, shivering)* Ach, Ursula! Es ist draussen sehr kalt. Bring unsere Mäntel!

URSULA: Sofort, Frau Knopf! *URSULA brings out two more long rectangles of fabric, die "Reisekleidung." The two women wrap themselves up and EXIT)*

DAS ENDE

WORTSCHATZ (in order of appearance in the play)

Sachen, die	*clothing articles*
anprobieren	*to try on (clothing)*
teuer	*expensive*
preiswert	*well-priced*
Reisekleidung, die	*travel clothes*
ausgezeichnet	*excellent*
weich	*soft*
Stoff, der	*fabric*
Rechteck, das	*rectangle*
Mode, die	*fashion*
berühmt	*famous*
Spiegel, der	*mirror*
lächerlich	*ridiculous*
spiegeln	*to reflect*
elend	*miserable*
Grösse, die	*size*

9. "Wir Kochen Heute mit Karl und Karoline"
🍎 Overview 🍎

SYNOPSIS: Karl und Karoline are the enthusiastic hosts of the wildly popular and moronic TV cooking show, "Wir Kochen Heute mit Karl und Karoline!" Join them today as they discuss and compare fruits as well as answer inane questions from their fervent, dim-witted studio audience.

> **LANGUAGE OBJECTIVES:**
> Vocabulary: fruits
> Structures: utility verbs in plural form, related to cooking

PRODUCTION NOTES:

This play pokes fun at both the hosts and studio audience of a TV talk show. Perform it in the irreverent tradition of a popular **Saturday Night Live** sketch.

Karl and Karoline always talk to each other and to the studio audience in overly excited and merry "talk show host" voice.

Naomi, Rolf, and Martin, as studio audience guests, hang on every moronic comment uttered by the show hosts, as if their remarks were priceless gems of knowledge.

IMPORTANT! Studio audience actors must always stand before they speak and sit down when they finish.

TO EXTEND THE LENGTH OF THE PLAY:

Add more members of the studio audience with idiotic questions.

Have Karl and Karoline introduce unusual tropical fruits such as the papaya, mango, guava, or kiwi.

TO REDUCE THE LENGTH OF THE PLAY:

Omit the dialogue regarding the strawberries and pineapple

STAGING SUGGESTION:

9. "Wir Kochen Heute mit Karl und Karoline"

CHARACTERS: 5 Actors
  KARL (*a wacky, exuberant cooking show host*)
  KAROLINE (*KARL's perky sidekick*)
  NAOMI (*a guest in the television studio audience*)
  ROLF (*also a guest in the television studio audience*)
  ULLI (*another lucky guest in the television studio audience*)

SETTING: *A sparkling TV kitchen: Karl and Karoline are situated behind a long table or countertop. Behind them a brightly colored sign announces the name of their TV show, "Wir Kochen Heute mit Karl und Karoline!" Also a row of at least three chairs that face the countertop for the studio audience of Naomi, Rolf and Ulli. The chairs should be set at a diagonal angle to the countertop, so as not to obscure the German class audience's view of the cooking show hosts.*

PROPS: *Karl and Karoline need aprons. A large bowl stands between them, containing red, green and yellow apples, an orange, a bunch of bananas, a lemon. Also a small bowl of green and purple grapes, a small bowl of strawberries, a pineapple, two cutting boards, two knives, two juice glasses.*

AT RISE: *KARL and Karoline, each wearing an apron, are either sitting or standing behind the sparkling kitchen counter with an attractive bowl of fruit between them. Wooden cutting boards and knives are placed before each of them. The studio audience, NAOMI, ROLF, and ULLI sit in chairs facing the cooking show hosts. They are applauding the start of today's show with great excitement and anticipation.*

KAROLINE: Guten Tag, Karl.

KARL: Guten Tag, Karoline, wie geht's dir heute?

KAROLINE: Es geht mir sehr gut, Karl. Danke. *(To studio audience)* Wie geht's euch heute?

NAOMI, ROLF, ULLI *(All whooping andly, adlibbing shouting raucous comments, such as)*: Sehr gut! Ich bin hungrig! Hallo, Karoline!

KAROLINE: Also, heute bin ich sehr aufgeregt,* weil wir heute eine neue Welt vom Essen entdecken werden.

KARL: Und, was ist diese neue Welt von dem Essen?

KAROLINE *(Mysteriously)*: Also, Karl, es ist etwas, dass du und ihr täglich* esst—zum Frühstück, zum Mittagessen, und auch zum Nachtisch. Es hat viele Farben, es ist süss, und hat viel Saft.* Weisst du, was es ist?

KARL *(Jovially baffled)*: Ich habe keine Idee, Karoline. Was ist es?

KAROLINE *(To studio audience)*: Wisst ihr es, mein liebes Publikum?

NAOMI, ROLF, ULLI *(Addlibbing, all shouting at the same time)*: Ich weiss nicht! Was ist es! Sind es Süssigkeiten?

KAROLINE: Ich spreche über Obst!*

NAOMI, ROLF, ULLI: *(Enthusiastic applause)*

KARL *(Slaps knee, laughing)*: Obst! *(Speaks to the TV audience with sudden seriousness)* Tatsächlich* ist Obst sehr wichtig für die Gesundheit. Karoline, hast du Obst gern?

KAROLINE: Natürlich habe ich Obst gern!

KARL: Isst du es jeden Tag?

KAROLINE: Ganz bestimmt!* Heute werden wir viele populäre Obstsorten in unserer Sendung, **"Wir Kochen Heute mit Karl und Karoline!"** gründlich* untersuchen.

KARL *(Confidentially)*: Ich muss dir sagen, Karoline, ich bin ganz aufgeregt.

KAROLINE: Ich auch, Karl. Schau mal, hier in unserem Korb gibt es viel Obst, das man im Supermarkt findet.

KARL: Zeig uns das Obst, Karoline!

KAROLINE: Sehr gern, Karl. *(To audience)* Und, wie immer, in unserer Sendung hören wir ihre Fragen und Bemerkungen* gerne an. Jetzt beginnen wir mit dem Apfel. *(Holds up red apple)* Hier ist ein Apfel. Der Apfel ist rot.

KARL: Karoline, sind Äpfel immer rot?

KAROLINE: Ach nein, Karl! Manchmal sind sie grün —

KARL: Ist das möglich?

KAROLINE: Ja, Karl! Und manchmal sind sie gelb.

KARL: Unglaublich!

9.3

ROLF: Ich hab' eine Frage, Karoline. Gibt es auch blaue Äpfel?

KAROLINE: Das ist eine gute Frage, aber nein, Äpfel sind nie blau. Sie sind immer rot, grün oder gelb.

ROLF *(Carefully mentally digests this information):* Gut. Danke schön.

KARL: Karoline, warte einen Moment! Was ist das im Korb? Ist das ein Apfel, der orangenfarbig ist? *(Picks up an orange)*

KAROLINE: Nein, Karl, das ist kein Apfel - das ist eine Orange. Die Orange ist sehr saftig. Schau mal, Karl, ich werde sie schneiden*. *(Cuts it in half)* Und jetzt mache ich Orangensaft. *(Squeezes some juice into a glass)*

KARL *(Drinks it):* Mmmm, er ist köstlich!* Ich habe den Orangensaft sehr gern!

NAOMI *(Importantly):* Karoline, zuerst muss ich dir sagen, dass mir deine Sendung sehr gut gefällt. Ich möchte dir auch sagen, dass meine Familie manchmal Orangensaft zum Frühstück trinkt.

KAROLINE: Das ist sehr gut. Wenn deine Familie es möchte, könnte sie auch Orangensaft am Nachmittag und am Abend trinken. Er schmeckt den ganzen Tag gut.

NAOMI: Wirklich? Das ist eine fantastische Idee! Danke, Karoline.

KARL: Karoline, ich sehe, dass es auch andere Früchte in dem Korb gibt. *(Chooses a lemon)* Das ist eine Zitrone, nicht wahr?

KAROLINE: Ja, das ist eine Zitrone. Die Zitrone hat Saft wie die Orange. Ich werde sie schneiden. *(She cuts it and squeezes some juice into a glass)*

KARL: Zitronensaft? Eine Limonade! Mmmm! Ich habe Limonade gern. Karoline, gib sie mir! *(He grabs the glass, Karoline grabs it away before he can drink the lemon juice)*

NAOMI, ROLF, ULLI: *(All roar with delighted laughter, applaud)*

KAROLINE *(Laughing):* Nein, nein, nein, Karl. Das ist noch keine Zitronenlimonade. Du musst Wasser und Zucker mit dem Zitronensaft zusammenmischen* wenn du Zitronenlimonade trinken möchtest.

NAOMI, ROLF, ULLI: *(Laughing uproarously)*

KAROLINE: Gut, Karl, was gibt's noch im Korb?

KARL *(Holds up banana):* Also, hier ist eine Banane. Weisst du, Karoline, dass man fast nie **eine** Banane kauft? Man kauft sie immer als Bündel.*

KAROLINE: Das ist sehr interessant, Karl!

9.4

ULLI *(Eagerly)*: Ich habe eine Frage; wenn man eine Banane mit dem Messer* schneidet, bekommt man Bananensaft?

KARL: Eine sehr gute Frage! Die Antwort ist "nein." Die Bananen haben wenig Saft.

ULLI *(Looks disappointed, confused)*: O.K., danke.

KAROLINE: Dann, was machen wir mit dieser seltsamen Frucht, Karl?

KARL: Man nimmt die Schale* weg, so macht man das — *(Demonstrates)* — und dann isst man sie.

NAOMI: Meine Tante in Amerika schneidet die Banane und dann isst sie die Banane zum Frühstück, mit ihrem Müsli* und Milch.

KARL: Eine wunderbare Idea! Karoline, wir lernen viel von anderen Kulturen, nicht wahr?

KAROLINE: Ganz bestimmt, Karl.

ULLI: Eine Freundin steckt eine Banane in ihre Tasche und isst sie nachmittags.

KARL: Ausgezeichnet!

ROLF *(Thinking hard)*: Kann man eine Banane vor dem Sport essen?

KARL: Natürlich. Gibt es andere Fragen?

NAOMI: Kann man eine Banane als Telefon benützen? *(Demonstrates)*

KARL *(Looks doubtful)*: Ich glaube nicht. Eine Banane hat keinen Strom.*

ULLI *(Jumps up, speaks excitedly)*: Ich weiss! Ich kann eine Banane in jedes Ohr stecken wenn ich nichts hören will! *(Demonstrates)* Ich höre nichts. Alles ist still!*

KARL: Hmm, vielleicht... *(Looks doubtful, then changes subject)* Karoline, gibt es noch andere Früchte in unserem Korb?

KAROLINE: Nein, Karl, darin gibt es nur Äpfel, Orangen, Zitronen und Bananen. Aber hier sind ein paar kleine Teller mit Obst.

KARL *(With disbelief)*: Gibt es noch mehr Obst? Ich kann das kaum glauben.

KAROLINE: Ja, Karl. Auf diesem Teller gibt es grüne und rote Trauben.*

ULLI: Was ist der Unterschied* zwischen grünen and roten Trauben?

KAROLINE: Der Unterschied ist die Farbe. Diese sind grün, und die anderen sind rot.

ULLI *(With sudden comprehension)*: Ach ja, jetzt verstehe ich es.

KAROLINE: Auf diesem Teller gibt es Erdbeeren. Diese Erdbeeren sind sehr schön. *(Confidentially)* Meine Lieblingsobst ist die Erdbeere.

NAOMI: Ich esse nie Erdbeeren, weil mir der grüne Teil sehr schlecht schmeckt.*

KAROLINE: Eigentlich sollst du den grünen Teil nicht essen.

NAOMI *(Excitedly)*: Wirklich? Ach, das ist gut. Danke vielmals. Ich werde **morgen** wieder Erdbeeren essen.

KARL: Es tut mir sehr leid, aber wir haben nur noch zwei Minuten in unserer Sendung, **"Wir Kochen Heute mit Karl und Karoline!"**

ROLF: Gibt es eine sehr grosse Frucht?

KAROLINE: Ja, du hast Glück weil ich eine hier habe. Sie ist die Ananas.*

ROLF *(Suspiciously)*: Ist das eine Frucht? Ist das nicht ein exotisches Tier?

KAROLINA: Sie ist eine Ananas und ja, sie ist eine Frucht. Sie ist eine Tropenfrucht und sehr populär.

KARL: Wir haben Zeit für nur noch eine Frage.

ULLI: Was mach' ich, wenn ich zum Supermarkt einkaufen gehe und kaufe viele Äpfel, Orangen, Bananen, Erdbeeren und Ananas, und ich möchte sie alle zusammen essen?

KARL *(His brow furrowed)*: Hmm. Das ist ein schwieriges Problem. Karoline?

KAROLINE: Kein Problem! In diesem Fall, kannst du sie alle schneiden und einen Fruchtsalat machen.

ULLI: Einen Fruchtsalat! Himmlisch! Danke vielmals!

KARL: Karoline, du bist die Königin* der Früchten. Ich weiss nicht wie du diese wunderbaren Ideen bekommst!

KAROLINE: Danke, Karl. *(She hands out fruits to cheering guests as Karl says his goodbyes and plugs next week's show)*

KARL: Nächste Woche, in unserer Sendung, **"Wir Kochen Heute mit Karl und Karoline!"** entdecken wir die geheime Welt von Reis. Grüss Gott! Und denkt immer daran, dass Früchte sehr wichtig sind! Auf Wiedersehen!

DAS ENDE

WORTSCHATZ (In order of appearance in the play)

aufgeregt	*excited*
täglich	*daily*
Saft, der	*juice*
Obst, das	*fruit*
tatsächlich	*as a matter of fact*
Sendung, die	*the program (TV)*
gründlich	*thoroughly*
bestimmt	*definitely*
Bemerkung, die	*remark*
schneiden	*to cut*
köstlich	*delicious*
zusammenmischen	*mix together*
Bündel, das	*the bunch*
Messer, das	*knife*
Schale, die	*peel (n)*
Müsli, das	*cereal*
Strom, der	*electricity*
Traube, die	*grape*
Unterschied, der	*difference*
schmecken	*to taste*
Ananas, die	*pineapple*
Königin, die	*queen*

10. *Ein Nachmittag mit Drei Freunden*
★ *Overview* ★

SYNOPSIS: Experience the delightful, mundane adventures of three friends one sunny afternoon.

> **LANGUAGE OBJECTIVES:**
> Vocabulary: adjectives
> Structures: comparatives and superlatives

PRODUCTION NOTES:

This play is written and should be performed in a surrealistic, rather two-dimensional style, different from all others in this book. The dialogue is highly repetitive, with the actors often reiterating the exact words of the narrator. The narrator should read from his or her script off to the side of the "stage."

IMPORTANT! The three actors, Peter, Paul, and Patrick, must overact; they must exaggerate all gestures, dialogue and expressions. They make eye contact with the audience whenever they speak. Again, the name of the game is surrealism!

No sets are necessary, however it is very effective to have either surrealistically painted backdrops (either simplistic, cartoonish, or in the style of the Impressionist painter, *Henri Matisse*) on sheets behind the performers to denote the different locations: a living room, a kitchen, a neighborhood street, and a park.

Props for the entire performance need to be placed within easy reach of the three friends before the play begins. They may be gathered together in an unobtrusive cardboard box or laundry basket.

TO EXTEND THE LENGTH OF THE PLAY:

The three friends meet three pretty girls, eerily similar in stature to the three boys, on their way to the park.

The three boys have little adventures on their way to the park. They pass mountains, zoos, beaches, all of which provoke much additional descriptive dialogue.

TO REDUCE THE LENGTH OF THE PLAY:

Omit the dialogue about the comical hats, or the singing.

10. *Ein Nachmittag mit Drei Freunden*

CHARACTERS: 4 Actors
    ERZÄHLER (a boy or girl narrator)
    PETER a boy (the "biggest," tallest, and oldest friend, also the most conceited)
    PAUL a boy (the "middle" friend)
    PATRICK a boy (the "smallest" friend)

SETTING: The setting for this play may be imaginary. Stdents may paint optional backdrops on sheets or butcher paper to represent: a living room, a kitchen, a neighborhood street, a park

PROPS: Seven sandwiches, three paper (lunch) bags, stuffed toy cat, magazine, TV remote control, mirror, three combs, three silly hats, a fake bee, a fake tarantula, a fake snake

AT RISE: *The three friends are sitting on the sofa. They are barefoot but their tennis shoes are nearby. PATRICK flips through a magazine, PAUL tosses a stuffed toy cat in the air and catches it, and PETER pushes a TV remote control. The narrator, ERZÄHLER, always stands off to the side, removed from the action, reading from his or her script.* **Optional livingroom backdrop hangs behind actors.**

ERZÄHLER *(In the bold, happy voice of a radio announcer):* Hier sehen wir drei Freunde. Wir werden sie kennenlernen. Dieser Junge heisst Peter. Peter ist jung. Er ist fünfzehn Jahre alt.

PETER *(Waves):* Hallo. Ich heisse Peter. Ich bin fünfzehn Jahre alt.

ERZÄHLER: Dieser Junge heisst Paul. Paul ist jünger. Er ist dreizehn Jahre alt.

PAUL *(Waves):* Hallo. Ich heisse Paul. Ich bin dreizehn Jahre alt.

ERZÄHLER: Dieser Junge heisst Patrick. Patrick ist der jüngste. Patrick ist zehn Jahre alt.

PATRICK *(Waves):* Hallo. Ich heisse Patrick. Ich bin zehn Jahre alt.

10.2

ERZÄHLER: Wie sind die Freunde? Ja, sie sind Freunde, aber sehr verschieden. Patrick ist gross.

PATRICK: *Stands up):* Ich bin gross. *(Sits down again)*

ERZÄHLER: Paul ist grösser.

PAUL *(Stands up):* Ich bin grösser. *(Sits down again)*

ERZÄHLER: Und Peter ist der grösste.

PETER *(Stands up, speaks boastfully):* Ich bin der grösste. *(Sits down again)*

ERZÄHLER: Die drei Freunde sind sehr nett.* Es ist ein schöner Nachmittag und die drei Freunde sind im Wohnzimmer. Patrick langweilt sich* und deshalb liest er eine Zeitschrift.*

PATRICK: Ich langweile mich und deshalb lese ich eine Zeitschrift.

ERZÄHLER: Paul langweilt sich auch und deshalb spielt er mit der Katze.

PAUL: Ich langweile mich auch und deshalb spiele ich mit der Katze.

ERZÄHLER: Peter langweilt sich auch und deshalb schaut er fern.

PETER: Ich langweile mich auch und deshalb schau' ich fern.

ERZÄHLER: Plötzlich* hat Peter eine Idee.

PETER *(Snaps fingers, looks at friends):* Ich hab' eine Idee. Gehen wir in den Park spazieren.* Wir können dort picknicken und dann Basketball spielen!

PAUL, PATRICK: Wunderbar! Gute Idee!

ERZÄHLER: Die drei Freunde laufen in die Küche und bereiten* das Picknick vor.

PETER, PAUL, PATRICK: *(Leave props on sofa, stand up, "run" to kitchen)*

ERZÄHLER: Peter bereitet vier belegte Brote* vor, weil er immer sehr hungrig ist.

Optional backdrop change to kitchen scene

PETER *(Holds up four sandwiches):* Ich bin immer sehr hungrig.

ERZÄHLER: Patrick bereitet zwei belegte Brote vor, weil er weniger Hunger hat.

PATRICK: Ich habe weniger Hunger.

ERZÄHLER: Und Paul bereitet nur ein belegtes Brot vor. Paul hat am wenigsten Hunger. Deshalb ist Paul der dünnste von den drei Freunden.

PAUL *(Holds up one sandwich):* Ich bin der dünnste von den drei Freunden . . . aber ich sehe sehr gut aus.

ERZÄHLER: Die drei Freunde geben die belegten Brote in Papiertüten.* Dann ziehen sie sich Schuhe an.*

PETER, PAUL, PATRICK: *(Place sandwiches in paper bags, put on tennis shoes)*

PATRICK: Meine Schuhe sind gross und neu.

PAUL: Meine Schuhe sind grösser und neuer.

PETER: Meine Schuhe sind die grössten und die neuesten. Meine Socken auch.

ERZÄHLER: Die drei Freunde müssen sich das Haar kämmen. Sie schauen sich im Spiegel an.

PATRICK *(As he combs his hair)*: Ich sehe sehr gut aus.*

PAUL *(As he combs his hair)*: Ich sehe besser aus.

PETER: *(As he combs his hair)*: Ich sehe am besten aus und bin auch sehr populär.

ERZÄHLER: Die drei Freunde setzen ihre Hüte auf.

PETER, PAUL, PATRICK: *(Put on silly hats)*

PATRICK: Mein Hut ist komisch.*

PAUL: Mein Hut ist komischer.

PETER: Mein Hut ist am komischten. Alle Leute haben mich gern.

ERZÄHLER: Die drei Freunde wollen spazierengehen. Peter ist ungeduldig.*

PETER: *(Crosses arms, taps fingers)*

ERZÄHLER: Paul ist ungeduldiger.

PETER: *(Taps foot, looks off scowling impatiently)*

ERZÄHLER: Patrick ist der ungeduldigste.

PATRICK: *(Paces)*

ERZÄHLER: Jetzt gehen sie, Peter, Paul, und Patrick, mit ihren Papiertüten und ihren komischen Hüten.

Optional backdrop change to neighborhood street scene

PETER, PAUL, PATRICK: *(Start "strolling" down street)*

ERZÄHLER: Sie gehen in den Park. Es ist ein schöner Tag und die drei Freunde sind sehr zufrieden.* Sie wollen singen.

PATRICK: Ich habe eine schöne Stimme. Ich möchte ein Lied singen. *(Sings a few bars of any song)*

PAUL: Ich habe eine schönere Stimme. Ich möchte auch ein Lied singen. *(Sings a few bars of a different song)*

PETER: Ich habe die schönste Stimme. Ich möchte auch ein Lied singen. *(Sings a few bars of a different song, adds smugly)*: Ich habe viel Talent.

10.4

Optional backdrop change to park scene

ERZÄHLER: Die drei Freunde kommen in dem Park an. Sie setzen sich auf den grünen Rasen*. Sie öffnen ihre Papiertüten und essen die belegten Brote. Die drei Freunde essen sehr schnell, weil sie Basketball spielen wollen. Aber, wie schade! Es gibt ein grosses Problem.

PETER, PAUL, PATRICK *(At the same time)*: Ach, wie schade! Wir haben ein grosses Problem. Wir haben keinen Basketball!

ERZÄHLER: Was werden sie jetzt tun?

PETER: Ich bin sehr sportlich; ich mache Übungen. *(He does some push-ups, then adds)*: Ich bin auch sehr stark. *(Flexes muscles)*

PAUL: Ich bin weniger sportlich. *(He does some jumping jacks)*

PATRICK: Ich bin am wenigsten sportlich, aber ich bin sehr intelligent! *(Puts on glasses, gets out calculator, does sums)*

ERZÄHLER: Plötzlich sieht Patrick eine Biene* im Rasen und schreit laut.

PATRICK: Aaaaaaa!

ERZÄHLER: Paul sieht eine grosse Spinne* im Rasen und schreit lauter.

PAUL: Aaaaaaaaaaaaaaa!

ERZÄHLER: Peter sieht eine Schlange* im Rasen und er schreit am lautesten.

PETER: Aaaaaaaaaaaaaaaaaaaaaa!

ERZÄHLER: Sie laufen aus dem Park.

PETER, PAUL, PATRICK: *(Start "running" in place with frightened expressions)*

ERZÄHLER: Patrick läuft schnell, weil er Angst hat.

PATRICK: Ich habe Angst.

ERZÄHLER: Paul läuft schneller, weil er mehr Angst hat.

PAUL: Ich habe mehr Angst.

ERZÄHLER: Und Peter läuft am schnellsten, weil er die meiste Angst hat.

PETER *(Yells hysterically)*: Ich will nicht sterben!* Mutti!

Optional backdrop change to back to livingroom scene

ERZÄHLER: Die drei Freunde kommen nach Hause. Sie setzen sich aufs Sofa und sagen nichts.

PETER, PAUL, PATRICK: *(Collapse on sofa, in same order amd position as AT RISE)*

ERZÄHLER: Peter ist müde* und summt* ein Lied.

PETER: *(Hums)*
ERZÄHLER: Paul ist müder und liest eine Zeitschrift.
PETER: *(Flips through magazine pages)*
ERZÄHLER: Aber Patrick ist am müdesten, weil Patrick . . . schläft.
PATRICK: *(Sleeping)*

DAS ENDE

WORTSCHATZ (in order of appearance in the play)

nett	*nice*
sich langweiligen	*be bored*
Zeitschrift, die	*magazine*
anschauen	*to watch*
plötzlich	*suddenly*
spazierengehen	*take a walk*
vorbereiten	*to prepare*
belegte Brot, das	*sandwich*
anziehen	*put on*
gut aussehen	*look good*
komisch	*funny*
ungeduldig	*impatient*
zufrieden	*satisfied*
Biene, die	*bee*
Spinne, die	*spider*
Schlange, die	*snake*
sterben	*to die*
müde	*tired*
summen	*to hum*

11. Frühstück für Fritz
● Overview ●

SYNOPSIS: Eva has the dubious pleasure of serving breakfast to Herr Hansen and his annoying "friend," Fritz.

LANGUAGE OBJECTIVES:
  Vocabulary: breakfast foods
  Structures: common phrases for ordering and dining out in a restaurant, use of auxiliary verbs (modals)

PRODUCTION NOTES:
  This play begins as a charming, friendly little breakfast scene and slowly descends into a lesson in frustration somewhere in the Twilight zone.
  Herr Hansen has a very demanding role, both in acting and in the large amount of dialogue he speaks. In the beginning he is just a regular guy having breakfast in a new restaurant. Gradually his eccentricities become more and more evident. Herr Hansen must believe that there really is a friend, "Fritz," sitting next to him.
  The food items should all be prepared and on the countertop at the beginning of the skit.

TO EXTEND THE PLAY'S LENGTH:
  Add more customers to the restaurant, seated at additional tables, all needing Eva's immediate attention.
  Add an additional waitress or a cook in the kitchen with whom Eva may commiserate.

TO REDUCE THE PLAY'S LENGTH:
  Omit the roles of Herr and Frau Frimel.

STAGING SUGGESTION:

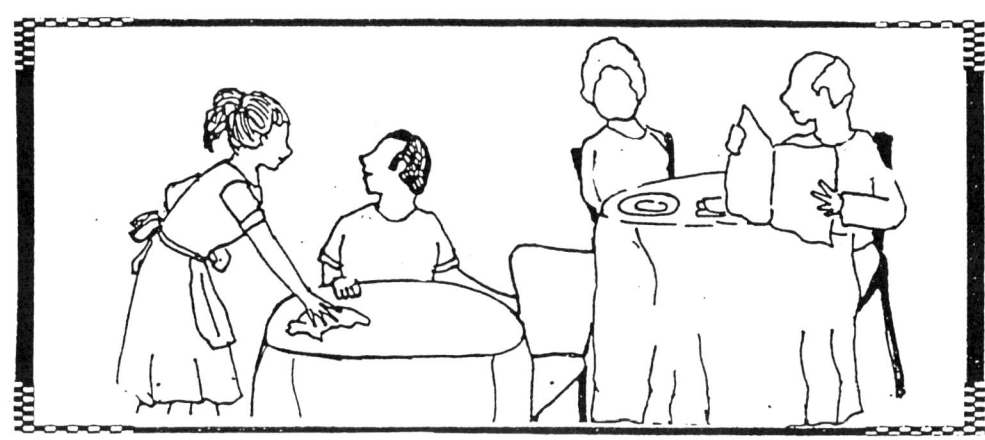

11. Frühstück für Fritz

CHARACTERS: 4 Actors
    EVA (a perky, down-to-earth waitress)
    HERR HANSEN (a friendly, but eccentric customer)
    HERR FRIMEL (a rather loud, nosy regular customer)
    FRAU FRIMEL (HERR FRIMEL's loud, pushy wife)

SETTING: The dining room of the restaurant "Eierspeisen," includes at least two 4-top tables (may be card tables with tablecloths), set with salt and pepper shakers, sugar packets, napkins and silverware, at least two chairs per table, a countertop near "kitchen" (which is located off-stage)
Optional backdrop: an attractive sign that says "Eierspeisen."
Also optional: posters that list today's special, kids' menus, etc.

PROPS: Table settings (see "SETTING" above), two menus, an order pad and pencil, a dinner plate with an omelet, toast with butter and marmelade, three bowls of oatmeal (one bowl must be <u>blue</u>). one glass of orange juice, coffee pot, two coffee cups & saucers, a newspaper, two glasses of water

AT RISE: *HERR und FRAU FRIMEL are seated together at their table, eating breakfast, drinking coffee, and reading the newspaper. HERR HANSEN enters the restaurant, looks around, chooses a table and sits down. EVA, with a pencil behind her ear and holding an order pad, walks over to his table.*

EVA *(In a perky, friendly voice)*: Guten Tag, mein Herr.
HERR HANSEN *(Congenially)*: Guten Tag.
EVA: Ich heisse Eva und ich bin Ihre Kellnerin heute. Willkommen in unserem Restaurant, **"Eierspeisen!"**
HERR HANSEN: Danke schön. Mir gefällt der Name Ihres Restaurants, **"Eierspeisen."** Ich nehme an Sie servieren allerlei Eierspeisen, richtig?

11.2

EVA *(Laughing)*: Natürlich. Alles ist schmackhaft.* Die Spiegeleier* sind besonders gut. Ich kann auch die Rühreier* empfehlen,* aber die Omeletten sind unsere Spezialität.

HERR FRIMEL *(Calls over)*: Noch eine Tasse Kaffee, bitte.

EVA *(Calls over to HERR FRIMEL)* Nur einen Moment, Herr Frimel. *(To HERR HANSEN)*: Ist das Ihr erstes Mal in unserem Restaurant?

HERR HANSEN: Ja. Ich wohne hier nicht. Ich bin auf Reisen.

FRAU FRIMEL *(Calls over)*: Mehr Toast und Butter, bitte.

EVA *(Calls back)*: Ich komme in einem Moment! *(To HERR HANSEN)* Möchten Sie ein Frühstück bestellen?

HERR HANSEN: Ja. Bringen Sie mir die Speisekarte,* bitte.

EVA *(Walks to counter, picks up menu)*: Hier ist unsere Speisekarte für das Frühstück. Alles auf der Speisekarte ist sehr gut.

HERR HANSEN: Danke, aber ich brauche zwei Speisekarten. Eine ist für mich und die zweite für meinen Freund.

EVA *(In a surprised voice)*: Ihr Freund? Es tut mir leid, aber ich sehe ihn nicht.

HERR HANSEN: Ja, ich reise* nicht gern allein. Ich reise immer mit einem Freund. Jetzt sind wir schon sehr hungrig!

EVA: Einen Moment, bitte. *(Gets coffee pot from counter, refills HERR FRIMEL's cup, brings toast and butter to FRAU FRIMEL, brings another menu to HERR HANSEN)* Eine Speisekarte für Ihren Freund.

HERR HANSEN: Danke, Fräulein. *(He opens menu, places it at the table setting next to him))*

EVA *(Gets two glasses of weater, returns to HERR HANSEN's table)*: Zwei Glas Wasser für Sie. Wo ist Ihr Freund? Ist er in der Toilette?*

HERR HANSEN *(Miffed)*: In der Toilette? Nein, er ist nicht in der Toilette! Hier ist er! *(Motions vaguely)*

EVA: Also dann, wollen Sie das Frühstück jetzt bestellen, or wollen Sie auf Ihren Freund warten?

HERR HANSEN *(Pleasantly)*: Wir wollen das Frühstück jetzt bestellen. Wir sind jetzt bereit.*

EVA *(Confused)*: Sie wollen jetzt bestellen? Ich sehe Ihren Freund noch nicht. *(Pauses)* Also, gut. Was wollen Sie essen?

11.3

HERR HANSEN: Ich möchte ein Omelett mit Schinken und Käse. Ein Omelett ist ja eigentlich ein Eierkuchen, nicht wahr?

EVA: Ja, das ist richtig.

HERR HANSEN: Ausgezeichnet!* Ich möchte auch zwei Stück Toast dazu.

EVA *(Writes on order pad)*: Sehr gut. Möchten Sie auch Marmelade oder Butter mit dem Toast?

HERR HANSEN: Ich möchte Marmelade **und** Butter. Was für Früchte servieren* Sie denn?

EVA: Heute servieren wir Pampelmusen,* Bananen, Melonen, und Erdbeeren.*

HERR HANSEN *(Pondering):* Ich werde keine Früchte essen. Gibt es Saft?

EVA: Wir haben Tomatensaft, Orangensaft, and Traubensaft.

HERR HANSEN: Sehr gut. Bitte bringen Sie mir ein grosses Glass Orangensaft.

HERR FRIMEL *(Waves coffee cup):* Fräulein, noch eine Tasse Kaffee, bitte.

FRAU FRIMEL: Mehr Toast mit Butter bitte, Fräulein.

EVA: Einen Moment! *(Turning to HERR HANSEN)* Wissen Sie, was Ihr Freund essen möchte?

HERR HANSEN: Nein, ich weiss nicht, was mein Freund essen möchte. Warum fragen Sie ihn nicht selbst?* *(Motions to empty chair beside him)*

EVA *(Cautiously):* Mein Herr, wo ist denn Ihr Freund? Ich sehe ihn nicht.

HERR HANSEN *(Explosively):* Gucken* Sie mal! Hier ist er, bei mir. Sehen Sie ihn denn nicht? Sie werden ihn beleidigen.* Was für eine lächerliche* Frage!

HERR und FRAU FRIMEL: *(Drop everything they're doing and stare at HERR HANSEN with total fascination)*

EVA *(Quickly, nervously):* Ach, nein! Ich will Ihren Freund nicht beleidigen.

HERR HANSEN: Dann sagen Sie ihm "Guten Morgen" und fragen Sie ihn, was er essen will.

EVA *(Looks at empty chair, speaks with an unsure voice):* Guten Morgen —Wie geht's Ihnen? Was wollen Sie heute zum Frühstück bestellen?

HERR HANSEN *(Listens to his invisible companion's answer, then gently argues with him):* Was sagst du? Du willst nur Müsli mit einer Banane? Nein. Du musst mehr essen. Ich bestehe darauf.* *(Listens)* Du hast kein Geld? Das macht nichts. Ich zahle die Rechnung* heute . . Schau her, wenigstens kannst du eine Schüssel Hafergrütze* essen. Kannst du das tun? *(Listens)* Gut, dann sag's der Kellnerin. *(Smiles apologetically at EVA, then* *talks again to invisible friend)* Warum willst du nicht mit der Kellnerin sprechen? Es tut mir leid, aber mein Freund will nicht mit Ihnen sprechen. Er möchte eine grosse Schüssel* Hafergrütze.

EVA: Ihr Freund möchte eine Schüssel Hafergrütze?

HERR HANSEN: Ja, bitte. Eine grosse Schüssel.

EVA: Sehr gut — Wie heisst Ihr Freund?

HERR HANSEN: Er heisst Fritz.

EVA: Aha —Fritz. Möchte Fritz Butter mit der Hafergrütze?

HERR HANSEN: Ich weiss nicht. Fritz, möchtest du Butter mit der Hafergrütze? *(Listens, nods)* Ja, Fritz möchte Butter. Was sagst du? *(Listens again)* Er möchte auch Zucker.

FRAU FRIMEL *(Calls over helpfully)*: Der Zucker ist auf dem Tisch.

HERR FRIMEL: Er ist neben dem Salz und dem Pfeffer.

HERR HANSEN: Danke.

EVA *(Consults her order pad)*: Also gut, Sie möchten ein Omelett mit Schinken und Käse und ein grosses Glas Orangensaft. Und Ihr Freund . .

HERR HANSEN *(Encouragingly)*: Fritz.

EVA: Ja. Fritz möchte eine Schüssel mit Hafergrütze und Butter.

HERR FRIMEL: Eine grosse Schüssel.

FRAU FRIMEL: Mit Zucker.

FÜNFZEHN MINUTEN SPATER

EVA: Hier ist das Frühstück. Ein Omelett mit Schinken und Käse, Toast mit Butter und Marmelade, und ein Glas Orangensaft. Passen Sie auf!* Der Teller ist sehr heiss. Und für —

HERR HANSEN: Fritz.

EVA: Ja, für *(Clears throat)* Fritz, eine grosse Schüssel Hafergrütze mit Butter. Guten Appetit! *(Exits to "kitchen")*

HERR HANSEN: *(Starts eating and drinking)*

FRAU FRIMEL *(Loudly, in a fake tone of voice)*: Ich gehe zur Toilette, mein Lieber. *(Stands and walks by HERR HANSEN's table, staring hard at Fritz's chair, exits)*

11.5

EVA *(Enters, returns to the HANSEN table)*: Schmeckt* Ihnen das Frühstück, mein Herr?

HERR HANSEN: Ja *(Wipes mouth delicately with napkin)*, mein Frühstück schmeckt mir sehr gut, aber Fritz hat sein Frühstück nicht gern.

EVA: Warum hat Fritz das Frühstück nicht gern?

HERR HANSEN: Fritz sagt, dass die Hafergrütze zu salzig ist. Fritz möchte eine andere Schüssel Hafergrütze.

EVA *(Enters, sets new bowl of oatmeal on HERR HANSEN's table)*: Hier ist eine neue Schüssel Hafelgrüze für Fritz. *(Waits expectantly, arms crossed)* Schmeckt ihm die Hafelgrüze jetzt?

HERR HANSEN *(Sheepishly:* Es tut mir sehr leid, aber Fritz sagt, dass diese Hafergrütze sehr kalt und nicht frisch ist.

EVA *(Takes offense)*: Die Hafergrütze in diesem Restaurant, **"Eierspeisen,"** ist ganz frisch, heute gekocht.*

HERR HANSEN *(Sternly to Fritz)*: Die Hafergrütze ist frisch, nicht alt. *(Listens)*

EVA: Was ist jetzt los? Was sagt Fritz?

HERR HANSEN: Fritz möchte eine andere Schüssel mit Hafergrütze.

EVA: Eine andere Schüssel mit Hafergrütze?

HERR HANSEN: Ja, bitte. Mehr Hafergrütze, aber dieses Mal in einer blauen Schüssel.

EVA *(Fuming)*: Wie Sie wünschen! *(Stomps off, returns with blue bowl, slams it on the table, waits)* Schmeckt ihm die Hafergrütze jetzt?

HERR HANSEN: Eigentlich nicht. Er sagt, dass die Hafergrütze in der blauen Schüssel unappetitlich* aussieht. Er sagt, dass er nicht mehr Hafergrütze essen will. Jetzt möchte er lieber Spiegeleier.

HERR FRIMEL *(Calls over)*: Die Spiegeleier sind ausgezeichnet!

FRAU FRIMEL: Auch mit Pfannkuchen!*

EVA *((Furiously)*: Geben Sie mir diese Schüssel mit Hafelgrüze!

HERR HANSEN *(Scolding)*: Hör mal, Fritz. Jetzt ist die nette Kellnerin böse. Du bist nie mit deinem Frühstück zufrieden. Immer machst du Probleme in Restaurants. *(Exasperated)* Was werde ich mit dir tun? *(Sighs, shakes head in resignation, then speaks to EVA)* Die Rechnung,*bitte.

EVA: Sofort!* *(Pulls bill off pad, gives it to HERR HANSEN)* Hier ist Ihre Rechnung.

11.6

HERR HANSEN *(Waves bill away, stands up, points to empty chair):* Geben Sie Fritz die Rechnung, bitte. Er macht so viele Probleme, dass **er** die Rechnung bezahlen soll. Danke vielmals. Auf Wiedersehen! *(HERR HANSEN exits purposefully, leaving EVA and HERR und FRAU FRIMEL motionless, mouths open in disbelief)*

DAS ENDE

WORTSCHATZ (In order of appearance in the play)

schmackhaft	*tasty*
Spiegelei, das	*fried egg*
Rührei, das	*scrambled egg*
empfehlen	*to recommend*
Speisekarte, die	*menu*
reisen	*to travel*
bereit	*ready*
ausgezeichnet	*excellent*
Pampelmuse, die	*grapefruit*
Erdbeere, die	*strawberry*
selbst	*yourself*
gucken	*to look*
beleidigen	*to offend*
blöd	*silly, stupid*
Hafergrütze, die	*oatmeal*
Rechnung, die	*bill*
Schüssel, die	*bowl*
hübsch	*pretty*
darauf bestehen	*insist*
aufpassen	*watch out*
gekocht	*cooked*
Pfannkuchen, der	*pancake*
sofort	*right away*
unappetitlich	*unsavory*

12. Hausarbeiten
✔ Overview ✔

SYNOPSIS: Mom requests help with the chores, but everyone in the family is too busy. Mom has the final revenge

LANGUAGE OBJECTIVES:
Vocabulary: chores to be done around the home
Structures: commands

PRODUCTION NOTES:
Mom may emphasize her bedraggled condition by wearing an old housedress and having her hair in curlers.

The living room should be rather messy. Scatter additional props from home around the living room set to augment this condition.

TO EXTEND THE LENGTH OF THE PLAY:
Add third child who does'nt want to wash/dry/fold laundry.
Add grandmother who does not want to wash the dishes.

TO REDUCE THE LENGTH OF THE PLAY:
Omit Mom's repetitive dialogue. (She always reiterates all the chores for the instructional purpose of reinforcement of vocabulary)

STAGING SUGGESTION:

12. Die Hausarbeiten

CHARACTERS: 4 Actors
    MUTTER (overworked, under-appreciated, but resourceful
    VATER (self-proclaimed king of the household)
    MONIKA, (their self-absorbed and mellow teen-age daughter)
    FRANZ, (their "all-American" eleven year old son

SETTING: A comfortable living room: contains a sofa, an armchair, a rug, a coffee table

PROPS: apron, list of chores, newspaper, vacuum cleaner, fingernail polish, broom, small radio/cassette player & earphones, building toy, duster, chocolate cake, one plate, knife, fork, napkins, various books, drinking glasses, bowl of popcorn

AT RISE: *As the play opens, the family is sprawled out in the living room. VATER lounges in the armchair reading the newspaper. MONIKA is settled on the sofa, polishing her nails. FRANZ is wearing earphones and listening to music while sitting on the rug and building something. Books, drinking glasses, and a bowl of popcorn are spread out on the coffee table. Some popcorn has spilled on the rug. MUTTER enters the living room, wearing an apron, holding a small vacuum cleaner, and looking harried.*

<u>NOTE</u>: *In this initial speech, MUTTER attempts to evoke a reaction from her family. She pauses expectantly after each sentence, but the family never responds or even acknowledges her.*

MUTTER *(Wearily)*: Ich bin sehr müde. Mein Rücken tut mir weh. . . *(Looks at each family member)*. Es macht mich müde, dieses Haus zu putzen. Ihr wisst, dass die Grosseltern uns morgen besuchen kommen . . . *(Turns to husband)* **dein** Vater und **deine** Mutter, **mein Liebling,** und sie besuchen nicht gern ein schmutziges Haus. . . *(Brightly)*. Also, wer möchte das Haus putzen? Ich habe eine Liste von Hausarbeiten* — *(Pulls list out of pocket, reads it)* Wir müssen den Boden kehren,* wir müssen staubsaugen,* wir müssen staubwischen* wir müssen die Papierkörbe ausleeren,* und dann muss ich endlich eine Torte backen. *(Sarcastically)* Hallo! habe ich eine Familie? *(Tries half-heartedly to clean table, sighs dramatically, turns to VATER)* Liebling, kannst du also bitte staubsaugen?

VATER *(Looks at MUTTER as if she were crazy)*: Ich? Staubsaugen?

MUTTER: Ja, du, mein Liebling, kannst du bitte staubsaugen?

VATER *(Self-important)*: Aber ich bin doch der Vater!

MUTTER: Ja, stimmt . . . und?

VATER: Ich bin der Mann in diesem Haus und ich muss mich ausruhen. Ich muss die Zeitung lesen. Das ist sehr wichtig *(He resumes reading)*.

MUTTER *(Moves newspaper with vacuum cleaner hose)*: Also, nimm schon den Staubsauger!

VATER: Wo soll ich denn staubsaugen?

MUTTER: Überall im Haus, aber besonders hier im Wohnzimmer, wo es sehr schmutzig ist.

VATER *(Looks at rug with spilled popcorn, looks back at MUTTER, speaks innocently)*: Das Wohnzimmer sieht nicht schmutzig aus. Es ist sauber *(Resumes reading the paper)*. Ich will dir gern helfen mit dem Staubsaugen, aber jetzt bin ich sehr beschäftigt. Vielleicht morgen . . .

MUTTER *(Wryly)*: Mein Mann will nicht staubsaugen. Nun, dann muss ich staubsaugen. *(Sighs, looks at list)* Meine liebe Tochter, Monika. Hier ist der Besen.* Kannst du bitte den Boden in der Küche kehren?

MONIKA *(Carefully painting her fingernails)*: Ja, Mutti, ich werde den Boden in der Küche kehren, aber jetzt geht es nicht *(admires nails)* Ich lackiere* gerade meine Fingernägel.

MUTTER: Aber, Monika, die Küche zu kehren dauert nur zehn Minuten. Bitte tu es doch.

MONIKA: Mutti, ich werde ja den Boden kehren, aber mein Nagellack* ist noch nicht trocken. Morgen kehre ich den Boden. Ich verspreche es dir.

MUTTER: Morgen ist zu spät. Morgen kommen deine Grosseltern zum Besuch. *(Sighs, very much the martyr)* Meine Tochter will den Boden nicht

12.3

kehren. Ich muss staugsaugen und auch den Boden kehren — Franz, mein lieber Sohn, willst du bitte die Papierkörbe ausleeren?

FRANZ: *(Rocks to music, builds a toy, doesn't hear his mother due to earphones)*

MUTTER: Franz, willst du bitte die Papierkörbe ausleeren?

FRANZ *(Still doesn't hear her)*

MUTTER *(Lifts up earphone and yells into his ear):* Franz, willst du bitte die Papierkörbe ausleeren?

FRANZ *(Startled):* Mutti, du erschreckst* mich!

MUTTER *(Softly):* Franz, willst du bitte die Papierkörbe ausleeren?

FRANZ: Welche Papierkörbe?

MUTTER: Die Körbe* in der Küche, in den Badezimmern, im Schlafzimmer, im Wohnzimmer...

FRANZ: Aber, Mutti, das sind ja nicht meine Papierkörbe!

MUTTER: Das macht nichts.

FRANZ: Wirst du mir dafür zahlen?

MUTTER: Du sollst dich schämen*! Das ist die einzige Hausarbeit die du zu Hause machst!

FRANZ *(Quickly, placatingly)* Mutti, ich werde gern die Papierkörbe ausleeren. Mit Vergnügen! Aber —

MUTTER: Aber was?

FRANZ: Ich möchte die Musik ein bischen länger anhören und weiter spielen. Aber später, Mutti. Ich verspreche dir. Später leere ich die Papierkörbe aus.
(He happily resumes listening to his headphones and building)

MUTTER: Mein Sohn wird die Papierkörbe nicht ausleeren. **Ich** muss es tun. **Ich** muss staubsaugen. **Ich** muss den Boden kehren.

VATER *(Distractedly, without looking up from newspaper):* Danke vielmals, mein Liebling.

MUTTER *(Glares at VATER, consults list again, then asks with false gaiety):* Wer möchte staubwischen? Das ist sehr einfach.* Man nimmt einen Staubwedel* *(Picks up duster from coffee table and demonstrates with exaggeration and sarcasm),* man staubt die Tische — die Stühle — die Lampe —das Gesicht meines Sohns ab!

FRANZ: Mutti! *(Reacts as she tickles his face with duster)*

MUTTER: Und man staubt das Sofa — und die Nägel meiner Tochter ab!
(Wipes Monika's hands with duster)

MONIKA: Mutti, meine Nägel!

MUTTER: Und man staubt den Sessel — die Bücher — und Vatis Zeitung ab!

VATER: Mein Liebling, bitte! Ich möchte die Zeitung lesen! *(They all resume inert positions)*

MUTTER: Also, verstehe ich alles gut? **Mutter** muss staubsaugen und den Boden kehren. **Ihr** müsst euch ausruhen. **Mutter** muss die Papierkörbe ausleeren und abstauben. Und wieder, **ihr** müsst euch ausruhen. **Mutter** muss eine Schokoladetorte backen . . .

VATER *(looks up abstractedly, oblivious to her ranting)*: Liebling, bring mir bitte eine Tasse Kaffee.

MUTTER: Ach, was für eine feine Familie habe ich! Ich bin müde! Ich backe eine Schokoladetorte. *(Exits)*

EINE STUNDE SPÄTER

MUTTER enters, humming contentedly, carrying a beautiful cake, one plate, one knife, one fork and one napkin. The family watches her every move. She carefully places cake on table, sits down, spreads napkin on lap, and proceeds to cut a slice of cake and savor each bite slowly. The family gathers around her attentively.

VATER: Mein Liebling, was für eine gute Bäckerin du bist! Gib mir bitte ein Stück Schokoladetorte.

MONIKA: Mutti, meine Nägel sind jetzt trocken. Gib mir bitte ein Stück Schokoladetorte.

FRANZ: Ich bin hungrig, Mutti. Gib mir bitte ein Stück von deiner Schokoladetorte.

MUTTER: Es tut mir leid, mein Liebling. Du musst doch die Zeitung lesen. Und Monika, eine Gabel wird sehr gefährlich für deine Nägel sein. Und Franz, wenn du ein Stück Schokoladetorte isst, kannst du nicht auf die Musik genug

12.5

aufpassen *(Savors another bite of cake)* — Wisst ihr was? Ich gebe euch einen Rat.* Wenn ihr Schokoladetorte essen wollt, geht dort in die Küche. Viel Glück! Diese Torte gehört mir!

DAS ENDE

WORTSCHATZ (in order of appearance in the play)

Hausarbeiten, die	*chores*
kehren	*to sweep*
staubsaugen	*to vacuum*
staubwischen	*to dust*
ausleeren	*to empty*
Papierkorb, der	*wastepaperbasket*
lackieren	*to polish (nails)*
Boden, der	*floor*
schämen, sich	*feel ashamed*
einfach	*simple*
Staubwedel, der	*duster*
Rat, der	*advice*

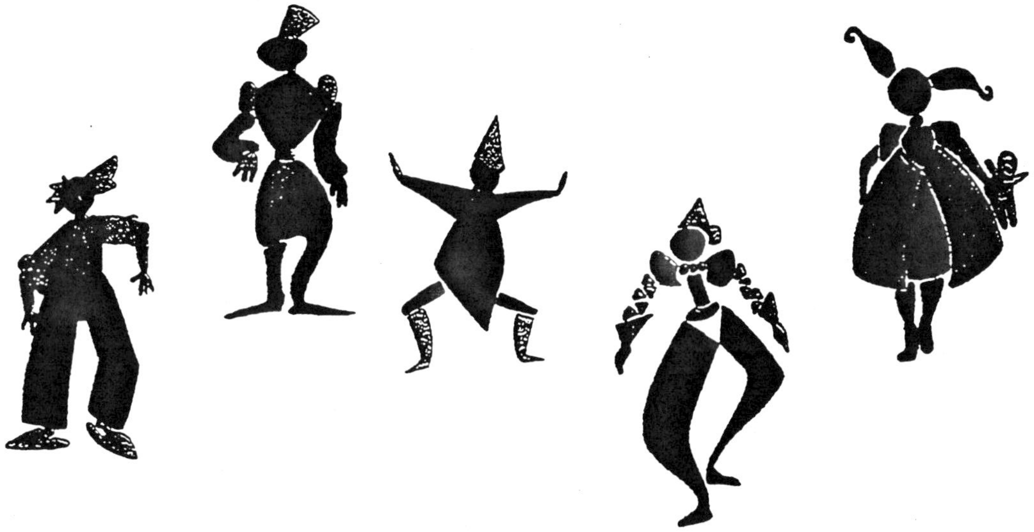

The Magic of Music and Theater in the Language Classroom

Workshops by Patti Lozano

Patti Lozano is a television teacher in Houston, and a well-known author, composer and national language consultant for several publishers.

Her energetic innovational workshops may include:

✿ *Chanting innovations and techniques*
✿ *Creative activities with flashcards and manipulatives*
✿ *Improvisation*
✿ *Role-playing*
✿ *Choreography to enhance language retention*
✿ *Total Physical Games*
✿ *Storytelling strategies*
✿ *Songs to enhance grammatical concepts*
✿ *Drawing activities*
✿ *Communicative and paired activities derived from songs*
✿ *Listening comprehension boosters*
✿ *Exploration of legends and cultures*
✿ *Acting techniques/bringing a script to life*

Request examples in Spanish, English, French and/or German
✓ Elementary, Middle or High School

Design and customize the workshop that will bring the maximum benefit to your classes and teachers!

For more information call: Dolo Publications, Inc.
Patti Lozano   PH: 281/463-6694
E-mail: dolo@wt.net OR plozano@swbell.net
FAX: 281/463-4808

Information and Order Page

Dolo Publications, Inc.
18315 Spruce Creek Drive
Houston, TX 77084
Email: dolo@wt.net

Tel. (281) 493-4552 or
(281) 463-6694
FAX (281) 679-9092
www.dololanguages.com

Send check, Charge, FAX or Purchase Order to above address, or Call Toll-Free **1-800-830-1460** to place an order.

Item No.	Description	Unit Price	Total
MS1	Music That Teaches Spanish - Book and CD	$31.95	
MM2	More Music That Teaches Spanish - Book and CD	$31.95	
ME5	Music That Teaches English - Book and CD	$31.95	
MF7	Music That Teaches French - Book and CD	$31.95	
MG9	Music That Teaches German - Book and CD	$31.95	
LC3	Leyendas con Canciones! - Book and CD & Activity Masters	$31.95	
LAL11	Latin-American Legends: On Page, on Stage and in Song - Book and CD	$31.95	
SGS8	Spanish Grammar Swings! - Book and CD	$31.95	
WT	Winzige Theaterstücke	$25.95	
PS4	Mighty Mini-Plays for the Spanish Classroom	$21.95	
PF4	Mighty Mini-Plays for the French Classroom	$21.95	
PG4	Mighty Mini-Plays for the German Classroom	$21.95	
PE4	Mighty Mini-Plays for the ESL Classroom	$21.95	
GT6	Get Them Talking!	$21.95	
CHAT	Let's Chat!	$24.95	
SS	Skinny Skits (in Spanish)	$24.95	
PPT	Petites Pièces de Théâtre	$24.95	
	Sub-Total		
	Shipping & Handling 10%, $5.50 minimum		
	Add 8.25% sales tax when applicable		
	Total		

Manner of Payment: Check_____ Charge _____ Purchase Order # _____

Name: _____

School: _____ District: _____

Address: _____

City: _____ State: _____ Zip Code: _____

Charge Card Information:

Cardholder Name _____

Street Address _____

City _____ State _____ Zip _____

Phone H: (_____) _____

Credit Card Number: (VISA or Mastercard Only)

Expiration Date ____/____/____ (include last 3 numbers on signature strip _____

NOTE: School districts, please enclose Purchase Order. Allow 2-3 weeks delivery.